LOOSE RELATIONS: YOUR IN-LAWS AND YOU

Also by Terri Apter

Fiction
SILKEN LINES AND SILVER HOOKS
ADONIS' GARDEN

Non-fiction
THOMAS MANN: The Devil's Disciple
VIRGINIA WOOLF: A Study of her Novels
FANTASY LITERATURE: An Approach to Reality
WHY WOMEN DON'T HAVE WIVES: Professional
Success and Motherhood

LOOSE RELATIONS

Your In-Laws and You

Terri Apter

MACMILLAN

First published 1986

Published by
THE MACMILLAN PRESS LTD
Houndmills, Basingstoke, Hampshire RG21 2XS
and London
Companies and representatives
throughout the world

Printed in Hong Kong

British Library Cataloguing in Publication Data
Apter, T. E.
Loose relations: your in-laws and you.
1. Parents-in-law
I. Title
306.8'7   HQ755.8
ISBN 0–333–37357–X (hardcover)
ISBN 0–333–37358–8 (paperback)

To David and Christine

Contents

Acknowledgements   ix
Introduction   xi

1   Confessions of a Daughter-in-Law   1
2   What is an In-Law?   9
3   What Has Marriage Got to Do With In-Laws?   21
4   My Spouse, My Self   43
5   How the Innocent Become Outlaws: The
    Transition from Parent to In-Law   63
6   Claustrophobia: In-Laws versus Self-Identity   87
7   Similarity and Harmony   105
8   Living In/Moving Out   123
9   The Birth of Grandparents   139

    Notes and References   157
    Selected Bibliography   161

Acknowledgements

I wish to thank all the people who spoke to me about themselves and their in-laws, and took the time and energy to discover what was going on behind the screen. I am also indebted to Dr Sandy Robertson for opening my eyes, and then directing them, to the wealth of anthropological quirks relevant to my subject. Dr Ray Abrahams of Churchill College, Cambridge, was also helpful in this respect. For specific cases of in-law troubles, I am grateful for the information provided by Philippa Comber of Churchill College, Cambridge, Stephen Barber and Jan King. Professor Scarlett Epstein and Swasti Mitter of the University of Sussex put some useful reading material my way, as did Bina Agarwol of Delhi University. For more general discussion I owe Merle Lipton, Dr Mary Polkinghorn, Dr John Polkinghorn, as well as Ann Duncan and Jean Gooder of Newnham College, Cambridge a large debt. I must thank, also, Anne-Lucie Norton of Macmillan Press who was responsible for the germination of the book, which soon came to seem inevitable. Finally, I wish to thank my parents-in-law, on whose generosity and capacity for forgiveness I am staking a huge bet.

T. E. A.

Introduction

Whenever I mentioned that I was writing a book about
in-laws, people laughed. They were not laughing at me, but at
the subject, which is surrounded by a conspiracy of humour.
The next question, invariably, was, 'Are you writing it under
your own name?' They immediately, and correctly, supposed
that I would be expressing my own feelings, and that my own
feelings were negative, for there was an appalled 'Really?'
when I replied that it would indeed be published under my
own name.

The reason for their concern, initially, is obvious. The book
does, after all, take skeletons out of the dining-room cupboard
and make them dance. But others' nervousness (on whose
behalf?) is less understandable when one considers how many
books do precisely that – they go beyond politeness, even
beyond consideration. Many writers have held their own
parents up to public ridicule, not for the sake of revenge, but
for the sake of understanding. Embarrassment is not a writer's
indulgence. Why, then, were people so ready to be em-
barrassed for me, and both amused and amazed at the notion
of being frank about my in-laws?

Most adults have in-laws, and many adults have problems with them, yet no one is writing about them. There is an agreement not to take such problems seriously, to joke about them without giving them any thought. Yet my own position demanded thought. My parents-in-law are without reproach, but my feelings are stereotypically hostile. The discrepancy between emotion and cause was too great to ignore. No one could help me understand it. The closest one comes to discussion about in-laws is in grouch sessions, where complaints are sympathetically swapped. I could not justify any complaint, and so I was left brooding on an apparently senseless sense of grievance. Finally, I wrote this book because I myself wanted to read it.

I did not think that a survey of what percentage of married couples have in-law troubles, or a demographic study of which groups tend to have them most, would be pertinent, and in any case they were beyond my abilities and my resources. It was already clear that in-law problems were common enough to be seen as typical. One didn't have to prove that they exist, even though many people do not experience them. Nor did any general theory about in-law clashes (were they primitive battles over territory or possession? were they due to transference of libidinal feelings towards our parents, and then denial of them?) much help. It was the simple, commonsense groundwork that had to be done. A number of specific cases had to be observed and considered. What frustrations and complaints lay behind the typical clashes? How deep were the problems? Were they isolated, or did they emerge within the structure of family feeling and marital compromises, disappointments and loyalties? Did in-law complaints serve any purpose? Do people who dwell upon them, or instigate them, derive any benefit from them? Are such problems ever resolved? What makes them change? These were the questions that interested me.

We are often ashamed of our in-law troubles. They tend to reveal a less than best side of us. We may be irritable with in-laws, quick to find fault, quick to take offence, quick to offend. What makes matters worse, and increases our shame, is that we are isolated within our own families in regard to these problems. Our spouses are bonded to our in-laws by blood, as are our children. We alone look upon them as outsiders. Ashamed and isolated, we tell inept jokes or utter sulking complaints. The idea of taking ourselves seriously is strange, disturbing, but liberating – hence it is amusing.

We are accustomed, these days, to view our love and hate, our anger and frustration, as complex and ambivalent. We know hatred and anger towards others contain within them images of our own doubts and failings and fears. We know our love is imperfect, as is our self-love, and often requires props. We know we seek decoys for self-dissatisfaction, and scapegoats for unacceptable desires. It is time some of this sophistication was turned towards our problems with in-laws. The subject, then, will no longer be funny, but fascinating.

T. E. A.

1
Confessions of a Daughter-in-Law

'Did you have a nice Christmas?'

She shrugged. 'It was lovely to see the children, but his wife takes exception to everything I say. Everything. I only have to open my mouth . . . '

I did not need to overhear anymore of this stranger's conversation to know she was referring to her daughter-in-law. I saw a hundred failed attempts to make friends. I saw her swallow insults in the hope that things would improve. I saw her try to forgive, and then grow sullen as she knew she would be judged wrong even before she spoke. I recognised the daughter-in-law's unrelenting attacks, alongside her shame. All this was crystal clear to me, because I am a daughter-in-law.

My parents-in-law give me no real grounds for complaint, and yet my feelings towards them are violent, hostile and

1

cruel. They are modest in their requests of me. They utter no complaint about me to myself or my husband or my children. Yet my ill will remains steadfast. Where does it stem from?

For many years I thought the problem was mine alone. My in-laws enraged me because I was unjust, possessive and ungenerous. But gradually I became aware that my own nastiness was readily matched by others where in-laws were concerned. As one woman explained, 'Normally I am reasonable with other people. Normally I try to be fair. I am quick to see others' virtues, and to appreciate what they are. But in regard to my parents-in-law I have a huge lapse of character. I don't know what their good points are.'

The most vehement objections to in-laws are often totally unsupported by specific criticisms. What did this woman's parents-in-law do to eclipse her good nature?

'They watch me', she said, after a pause. 'They come to visit and they sit and watch me. They watched me get ready to come here tonight. They'll watch me when I come home, and they'll watch me until they leave.'

What war was being enacted by this sullen staring? Was the mother-in-law trying to understand the woman whom her son loved, but who obviously hated her and despaired at her own hatred? Was she mocking, or criticising, or perhaps pleading silently? Why was irritation so quick to rise to the surface, when its causes remained obscure?

Repeatedly, indeed regularly, people apologised for their complaints about in-laws, dismissing them as 'petty'. They would begin with an outburst against an in-law and then counter their emotion by saying, 'But I have nothing against her/him, really', sometimes adding, 'She just gets on my nerves', 'She happens to drive me up the wall', or, with humour of which they seemed quite unaware, 'I just wish I could get as far away from her/him as possible.'

We are dealing with a very difficult situation – that of being 'son' or 'daughter' or 'mother' or 'father' but at the same time not being one. The family terms are hardened by 'in-law' – or is the coldness of 'in-law' softened by the prefix of the family terms? What do we want of them, or they of us? How do we fail them – or fear that we fail them, as we sense them watching us with an outsider's eyes and an insider's knowledge? How do they fail us – as indeed they do, since our annoyance signals demands unmet, and our anger underlines countless disappointments? From where do these grotesque expectations, which allow hatred to breed, arise? Why do we cling to them so long after we have learned their uselessness?

There are many answers which I will look at in this book. Each story has its own twisted logic and its own hidden reasons. My in-law problems do not arise in a vacuum, but continue on from my family history. Memories of my mother are of darting eyes which seek out every flaw and find crippling character defects in the tiniest weakness. She was a maternal giant who distrusted me, sought possession of me, feared me and helplessly loved me. These memories coexist with an overwhelming regret at having lost her, and a compulsion to relive endlessly the suffering of her final illness, as a means of dulling the terror of her death. I can find no bridge between my love and compassion on the one hand, and my image of an ogre on the other. Nevertheless I am protective towards this dark image, and resent my mother-in-law because she denies it – not directly, of course, but through the myriad of assumptions that govern her responses and determine her emotional vocabulary. Thus it is her very sweetness that enrages me, as it ignores the quality of my own psychological history, and hence invalidates me. I feel isolated and humiliated because I know my feelings could never gain admission to her consciousness. I am reduced to a paranoid adolescent and, like an adolescent, wish I could impress her with my adult individuality.

The dual position of being 'daughter' but a stranger, a 'daughter-in-law', creates a crucial difficulty. I cannot fault her as a mother. I love both her children – my husband and sister-in-law – and I see how their generous natures, their spontaneity and enthusiasm, their resilience, their loyalty and their capacity for unquestioning attachment, developed within the compass of her optimism. She believed that her children would be nice, and that the world would be nice to them. Her assumptions and manipulations somehow worked for them, and they are able to cope with the pressure of her sweet vision, displaying their different outlooks in bouts of teasing – which she controls very well, because she concentrates on the fun they mean to have, rather than their purpose. I, as an outsider, cannot tease her; but then, as an outsider, I should not need to. I should not feel bound by her tight network of assumptions and therefore should not fight it. But I am not simply an outsider to her, and therefore she must work extra hard to mould me in an acceptable image, and to control or deny the unacceptable in me; and she is not simply an outsider to me, but the shadow of a mother, and so I feel the pressure of her projected image, which makes me feel rejected, worthless and furious. I am being cast out to make way for a model that will suit her. This insult makes me see her as depriving and controlling and powerful.

Whom do I think she wants me to be? My first brother-in-law was her ideal child-in-law. He was slightly built, soft-spoken and successful. He was English, Protestant and required no explanation or apology. In contrast I am a foreigner and a Jew, someone they do not want to know or understand. When their model son-in-law began to treat their daughter abominably, however, I gained some advantage. My mother-in-law's recognition of me went to surprising lengths. She temporarily honoured my request to address me by my own, rather than by my husband's name. She temporarily heeded my requests to control my children's diet when they visited her. She temporarily heard my answers to her queries. I think she realised she could not control her children-in-law, and therefore she was compelled to respect their terms of reference. My second brother-in-law reinforced her fear, and has stood me in good stead. He is a joy. Large and loud, with an uncontrollable temper, he unwittingly shocks our parents-in-law at every turn. He is far more generous in thought towards them than I, yet he causes them far more distress because his flashes of anger and gloom cannot be ignored as can my morose resentment. I envy his ability to force them to recognise his difference and his danger.

What I want from my parents-in-law – what so much of this hostility is about – is recognition of me on my terms. But why should they grant this? Why should they relinquish their moderate English consciousness to acknowledge a first-generation American, with immigrant uncertainty hot at her heels, steeped in a psychological folklore based on isolation, fear, ambition and naïvety? Why should they do this as long as they are in control? And they are adept at maintaining control. The more I try to shock them into recognition, the stronger their defences become. At times my mother-in-law literally does not hear what I say, and in her presence I feel like a ghost, acting within a setting that is real, but in which I have no reality.

My own mother viewed me as a dangerous object which could be controlled only by a gargantuan maternal will. Unless she fought me, I would destroy myself. Unless she pinned me to the ground with her verbal abuse, I would not understand the world and my proper place in it. My mother and my mother-in-law, then, are not simply different, but have in my mind become perfectly matched opposites. My mother's hysterical concern for me had a ridiculousness you could really get your teeth into. There was passion behind the cruelty, and a sense that something of overwhelming value was at stake. With her vision of sweetness and light, with her confident control and power and righteousness, my mother-in-law has become my anathema. Here is my mother's true match, a person who can limit me and redefine me, but for her own good, not mine.

There is also a more general, less personal objection to her, which is shared by many women of my generation towards women of her generation. For she haunts us with the compulsion to make others happy, to do everything for others, to manipulate people by making them indebted to her, to prove her importance by creating dependencies. At the stressful dinner hour, when I face the transition from worker to house-wife, while I prepare a meal and cater to attention-starved children, her image haunts me, and I see her rushing about her own kitchen, playing the martyr and demanding gratitude from all. The strange thing is that I am competing with my mother-in-law while pretending to disown the roles she adopts. Here I am, trying to meet my family's endless demands, while ruling the house according to my wishes and simultaneously thinking that my family should be eternally grateful to me. I summon up my mother-in-law's presence to witness my business and my competence, and while summoned, she is arraigned for the type of woman she – and I, at this moment – represent.

My mother-in-law, then, is the innocent scapegoat for my own feelings towards my mother. She becomes the object of my anger, of the threats to annihilation we all first experience at the hands of our mothers, upon whom we depend and who invariably let us down, because our demands are so great. I am able, because so much resentment is directed towards my mother-in-law, to accommodate my love for my mother, to see her love for me in her often grotesque behaviour, and even to judge her to be right and good. In addition, my mother-in-law becomes a scapegoat for any failing I find in my husband. If he is too demanding of me in a domestic role, then it is his mother who is responsible for his presumption and dependence; but his good qualities are all his own. Finally, she becomes a scapegoat for my role as household martyr, which I adopt and yet in which I do not believe. It is her image, I feel, being injected into me, and is not properly mine. What a useful thing a mother-in-law is!

Whether we 'get on' or not with our in-laws has little to do with how well our personalities are matched, or how many interests we share. Family relationships – even tenuous ones outlined by law rather than by blood – are very different from friendships. Whatever the quality and character of an in-law relationship, it is never simple, but part of a larger network which will include one's attitude towards one's own parents, or towards one's child, or towards one's self and one's particular needs of confirmation and consideration within the family. 'My mother was famous and extraordinary', Alexandra told me, 'but I like my mother-in-law because she is ordinary, and doesn't make me feel so pale in contrast.' The mother-in-law is appreciated as the opposite of the mother, providing relief from the competition of the mother's achievements. Her affection is not based on simple compatibility, but has a much larger frame of reference. Nor, for those lucky few who love their in-laws because someone whom they love loves them, is affection based upon personal compatibility but on one's attachment to a spouse.

Problems with our in-laws are far more complicated than our successes. They have long been the subject of jokes – not because the conflicts are particularly funny, but because they involve feelings which we believe should be beneath us. So we either ignore these feelings by being extra nice and trying very hard to please our in-laws and to be pleased by them, or we pretend that the fault is all theirs, that they are sub-human, worthy objects of those worthless jokes. We barely know what is happening when that large family dinner, in which everyone is trying to show pleasure, breaks down with quarrels about politics or religion or the tone of one's voice or yesterday's price of beans. Our own arguments surprise us as much as those directed against us, because we are not quite sure what we are angry about, or we think we are mildly irritated when in fact we are furious. We are furious because the issues at stake are large – they involve self-recognition, possession, priority, our spouse's autonomy and the development of our marriage. These issues may be buried in small details, and we may be protected from them by in-law clichés, but the protection does us little good. The antagonism goes on and on because it never establishes its goal – because we do not see its goals. This book sets out to retrieve in-law problems from the emotional rubbish pit wherein they now lie, to make sense of them, and to grant them their proper due of pity and understanding.

2
What is an In-Law?

According to the sacred law of the Old Testament it is
unlawful to have sexual intercourse with near kin or 'to
uncover their nakedness'. But who are our near kin? Is one
allowed to marry a wife's sister or a stepmother, neither of
whom are related by blood? Augustine, concerned with the
delicate question of how to interpret 'near kin', wrote to Pope
Gregory, who replied that though, according to Roman secu-
lar law, first cousins can marry, the offspring of such marriages tend not to thrive, and therefore, according to Catholic
law, relations who marry must be at least three or four times
removed. During the Protestant Reformation some of the
extensive prohibitions were relaxed, but marriage to the
widow or widower of close kin, or to the siblings of a dead
spouse, was still forbidden, despite the absence of any scriptural authority.

These prohibitions indicated a change from earlier practices, and continuing practices in non-Christian societies. In
Ancient Israel a man was obliged to marry his dead brother's

wife – and no scriptural text queries this practice. In Ancient Greece a man was obliged to marry the daughter of. his father's brother if she was an heiress who had no brother. The oriental or Arab system of marriage is characteristically endogamous (marrying within a family). The most extreme example comes from Egypt, where the Roman censuses of the first three centuries A.D. show a remarkably high percentage of brother–sister marriages; but usually in this system the most desirable marriage is with the father's brother's daughter. This prevents the daughter's inheritance (which under Koranic law is half her brother's share of the family property) from being passed on to other families. For her children will be of her husband's family, and her wealth will be passed on to them; only if her husband belongs to her father's family, will the wealth remain within her family.

The whole of Europe, under the influence of the church, eventually rejected the 'logic' of marriages within the family. Protestants may have abandoned their formal opposition to cousin marriages, and the Catholic Church in 1917 modified its laws to exclude only first-cousin marriages, but prejudice against inter-family marriages remains strong.

The curious suffix 'in-law' added to the parallel kin of the spouse is clearly linked to the introduction of the Christian rules of marriage. The modification of such terms as 'father', 'mother', 'sister', 'brother' by the phrase 'in-law' indicates that from the standpoint of marriage, these relatives are kin in the eyes of the church. In law, these relatives are as mother, father, brother, sister, and marriage is not to be allowed; in law, they are close kin. The French and Dutch use a prefix of 'beau'/'belle', which also emphasises the close affinity in the eyes of canonical law, but it is more placatory than the English suffix, as though to remind one not merely of the prohibitions but of affection, too. In modern German a special morpheme is added to the family term to indicate affinity, but High German, which flourished before the influence of canonical law, has special terms for parents- and brother- and sister-in-law; and, significantly, Yiddish, unaffected by

Christian prohibitions, retains all the special terms for these relations from the Old High German.[1]

Why did the church place prohibitions on in-marrying, which had previously been customary, and which was beneficial to the maintenance of family property? The reasons the church gives are first, the moral reason, that marriage within the family would threaten the respect and shame due to near relations; secondly, the social reason, that distant marriages enlarge the range of social relationships; and thirdly, the reason we still hold to today, that the fertility of the mother or the health of the children might be endangered. Thomas Aquinas also raised the point that incest defies our 'natural and instinctive' feelings of honour towards our parents and close kin. Also, he suggested that if those who lived with us were sexually available to us we would become lustful and overindulgent. Montaigne believed that if family affections were joined to sexual love, the emotion would be so strong that people would lose their reason. But it is generally accepted by historians that the basis for these prohibitions was the church's desire to accumulate property. The princes of Europe were all related in some way, and therefore, if they wanted to marry one another without trangressing the canonical limits, they had to keep on good terms with the church and the court of Rome, to respect it and, above all, to make payments to it.[2] At a local level, the people of a largely in-bred village would have to make payments to have their marriages sanctioned. But more important, and more central, was the way the church made money out of heirlessness. If a girl could not marry within her father's family, the father might disinherit her rather than see his property go to stranger's children (she and her husband's children were virtually strangers to him in that they did not belong to his family), and then, if he had no sons, would leave his money to the church. If he did leave his money and property to his daughter, then the church would collect transfer and acquisition taxes[3] – though these were not necessary if the money was more 'naturally' passed on to the son.

11

Today, in Europe and America, the system of dowry and inheritance has given way to investment in upbringing and education of one's children. Thus the central and most common issues between in-laws do not involve property and wealth. Nor do they involve carrying out specific duties since, in our society, no specific duties are indicated by the in-law relationship. Parents generally make their own provisions for retirement and old age, relying upon their income, or the government, or their employer, rather than on their children and children-in-law. What then do we owe our in-laws? What do they owe us? What meaning does the relationship have today?

We owe our in-laws some kind of respect, some kind of deference, and perhaps we feel we should exhibit solidarity with them, as part of our family, but they are also very different from those members of our family who are related to us by 'blood', who share genetic material with us, with whom we have been associated from birth. Today the phrase 'in-law' does not so much indicate that someone is a mother or father or brother or sister in the eyes of the law; instead, it distinguishes those related by marriage from those who are natural relations. It signals difference from our natural relations, not similarity. It is a term of separation, not identity. Some people maintain that only natural or blood relations are true relations, and insist: 'No, she is not a relative; she is an in-law.'

This peculiar cold phrase can be suffixed to any relation of the spouse – one could speak of an aunt-in-law or a cousin-in-law; but in practice it is usually only tagged onto one's spouse's closest relatives – father, mother, brother, sister – or to one's children's spouses; though it is also used for one's sister- or brother-in-law's wife, which is actually a relation by marriage once removed. In-law relationships are of course more tenuous than blood relations. They depend upon the survival of the marriage. Children may be disinherited, and even disowned, but the parent who says, 'He is no longer my son', is stating something he knows cannot really be true. He makes a strong, cruel pretence, a determination to act as though the son were not his child. But we can, legitimately, have ex-in-laws, though it is more common for someone to think of his or her spouse's family as ex-in-law if the marriage has ended in divorce rather than in death. A widow will speak of her mother-in-law; a divorcee will speak of her ex-mother-in-law. The widow will want to feel she is still closely connected to her husband. She may feel loyal to her marriage. Her husband's death does not change her bond to his family. The divorced woman, as part of the psychological process of divorce, will see herself as separate from her husband and therefore as separate from her husband's family.

What do we Call Them?

The uncertainty about what our relations should be with our in-laws, and what type of deference or affection is owed them, is reflected in our uncertainty as to what to call them. We know we cannot call them by the term which defines their relationship. We can call our mother 'Mother', but we never, as far as I know, call our mother-in-law 'Mother-in-law'. Many people believe that parents-in-law should be treated like parents, and address them as 'mum', 'mom', 'ma', 'dad' or 'pop'; but they are careful to use different terms for their own parents. If a man calls his mother-in-law 'ma', he will call his own mother 'mum'. If parents-in-law insist upon being addressed by a parental term, the child-in-law usually complies, though may feel resentful. One woman said that she called her mother-in-law 'mum', but admitted 'it chokes me to say it.' Sometimes terms for parents and parents-in-law are distinguished by adding a Christian or family name. 'Mother Jones' or 'Ma Jane' indicate both relation and separation. Christian names are often used, and the children-in-law usually feel more comfortable with this practice unless they are under pressure from the parents-in-law to use a more familiar term. When the couple have children, the son- or daughter-in-law are usually comfortable calling the parent-in-law Granny or Grandad – addressing them by the names their children use. In conversation they are usually referred to as 'my mother-in-law' or 'your mother' or 'your grandmother'.

13

This type of reference, with the emphasis always on the in-law's relation to someone else, may paralyse the child-in-law into what Erving Goffman calls 'no-naming' or the zero form of address. Some people never address their mothers-in-law by any name whatsoever. They are able to get her attention with a little cough or clearing of the throat, or they are satisfied never to speak to her unless they have direct eye contact, so that addressing her by a name is unnecessary. When it is necessary to write to her they might add a post-script to the spouse's letter, thereby avoiding the question of what to put after 'Dear . . .' One person reported that under pressure to get his mother-in-law's attention he blurted out 'Mrs Hepburn!' though he had been married to her daughter for eight years. The formality stunned everyone in the room.

The problem is not reciprocal – parents-in-law tend to call their children-in-law by their Christian names, as they do their own children, and they usually refer to them as 'my daughter-in-law' or 'my son-in-law'. But the recent trend of women retaining their family surnames after marriage, can for some reason utterly confuse parents-in-law. One woman, a writer, told her mother-in-law that she was using her maiden name. 'You mean you'll write under your maiden name?', the mother-in-law tried to clarify. 'No, I'll be keeping my maiden name', the daughter-in-law insisted. 'Oh, can you do that?', the mother-in-law queried, but apparently accepted it. However, all letters were addressed to 'Mr and Mrs Hall'. All cheques, in lieu of presents, were made out to 'Mr and Mrs Hall' and they were always introduced as 'Morris and Alice Hall'. My own mother-in-law has been nagged by both me and my husband to accept that I use my maiden name, and the message gets across – temporarily. She will address letters to both of us, properly, for a week or so, and then will change to addressing us as in the conventional way or will try to wriggle out of her dilemma by addressing letters to the family in general. Perhaps she is insulted that I refuse to take her son's surname, which would make my formal name the same as hers, but I think her true concern is that the postman will think that a couple with different names are not properly married. However, all this pales to insignificance in face of the man who tried to pressure his daughter into taking her husband's name by remarking that in his will he had left nothing to anyone called 'Ms Marshall'. His daughter, by separating herself from her husband – or rather by using this method to individuate herself from her husband – was insulting her father, who saw the husband as representing masculine control over her.

False Relations

The confusion around the names we use to address in-laws is linked to our confusion about the relationship we have to our in-laws. Should they be like our parents are to us, or like our children are to us? Should we treat them as though they were parents or children to us, when they obviously are not?

In-law relations share with step-relationships the feature of being like a close relation, but without having any 'blood' or genes in common. The terms 'parent-in-law' and 'step-parent' were used interchangeably until the nineteenth century. In fact, the term 'parent-in-law' was not used until the fifteenth century, and the relationship now designated as 'in-law' was then called 'stepmother' or 'stepfather'. Therefore the folklore images of the cruel stepmother are also linked to images of the mother-in-law – the mother figure who represents a mother, but who is not one's true mother.

The classic tragedies of failed step-relations are well known. In fairy tales we see the stepmother who has the power of the mother, and the duties of a mother, yet who is not herself bound to the children as a mother is. Therefore, unlike a natural mother, she will put her need for food before that of the children (Hansel and Gretel), or will envy her daughter's beauty and seek to destroy it (Snow White), or will put the interests of her natural children above the interests and needs of a stepchild, making the stepchild servant to the natural children (Cinderella). These stepmother stories are often interpreted as representing the dark side of the mother.[4] For however much a mother loves her child, the mother is also a person, with the selfishness and self-interest of any person. The child knows this and fears this. Moreover, the child is also a selfish and self-interested person, however much he or she loves the mother, so that the child, too, resents the mother's power and beauty, and ignores the mother's physical needs. The child is aware of his/her anger and selfishness, and fears the mother's retaliation, or wants revenge upon the mother for her selfishness. The cruel fairy tale stepmother is a construction of the child's fear and anger towards his/her own mother. The hated aspects of the mother are split off from the loved aspects of the mother, so that on the one hand there is the stepmother, and on the other hand there is the fairy godmother. The function of the fairy tale is to allow the child expression of his/her anger, and the opportunity to tolerate his/her ambivalence.

The father who appears in these tales is usually the natural father. He is loving but ineffectual. Sometimes he is weak, and gives in to the nagging of the stepmother (Hansel and Gretel); sometimes he is ignorant of the stepmother's cruelty, and his ignorance is based upon infatuation with the stepmother (Snow White); and sometimes he has simply vanished from the picture (Cinderella). But the father and stepmother have to work in some sense as a pair. The stepmother is very different from a natural mother in that her power has to come via the father's weakness. At the time the fairy tales developed, stepmothers were far more common, because the death of young women, especially during childbirth, was more common, and therefore children would be raised by their natural fathers and their stepmothers. The stories show not only the child's split attitude towards his/her natural mother, they also quite clearly exhibit the possibilities, and perhaps some histories, of life with a mother figure who does not love the child as a mother.

Failed step-relations are widely recognised. What is less well known is the number of step-parents who are desperate to overcome the traditional image, and to prove their genuinely-felt love for the stepchildren. It is a difficult task, but it is a feasible one. They wish to represent the natural

16

parents in so far as they can. They wish to take the parent's place without degrading or denying the child's attachment to his natural parent. But what is the goal of someone who wishes to be a good parent-in-law? How can a parent-in-law put his or her child-in-law's interests and needs on the same level as his or her own child? There are cases in which the parents-in-law feel they are like parents to a child-in-law, usually when the child-in-law's parents are dead, or when they have no child of that sex themselves. There are some happy instances of in-law relations, but there are few guidelines, and many confused expectations. The parent figure who is not a parent inherits the distrust we have of the step-parent. The parent-in-law presents us with a similar doubt and a similar dread – are we to be aliens, or do we confront aliens, within our own family?

The important difference between a stepmother and a mother-in-law is that the mother-in-law usually has far less power than the stepmother, who inherits the mother's position in the home and with the father. However, in India, where the mother-in-law does have great power within the home, and over the bride, tales more gruesome even than that of Hansel and Gretel have recently emerged.[5] 'Dowry deaths' – killing by fire (claimed to be caused by an oven exploding) and falling from windows (claimed to be accidents or suicides) and stabbing, have been instigated by a bride's in-laws because her family cannot keep up with the dowry payments promised at her marriage. It is easier to kill the daughter-in-law than return her to her family, because if she were returned then the payments which had already been made would also have to be returned. Even when the behaviour falls short of the criminal, relations between the mother-in-law and daughter-in-law in India tend to be troubled because the mother-in-law does have power, and power makes in-laws ruthless.

Outsiders

Are in-law problems peculiar to Western society, in which the choice of a marriage partner is left to the couple themselves,

17

and an in-law is foisted upon, not chosen by, the rest of the family? It seems not. Marriage itself, which brings in-laws, also carries with it in-law problems. Roughly, the institution of marriage is a means of preserving the family – its name, its property, its children. But to reproduce the family, which is to preserve it, incest must be avoided. And if incest is to be avoided, then an outsider must be brought into the family, thereby threatening the very integrity marriage is meant to preserve. Some societies find this threat intolerable. Should their wealth be passed on to children whose allegiance is divided between two families? Should their power or prestige be shared by another family? Should their customs and interests and beliefs suffer the influence or criticism of an outsider? To avoid these conflicts, they toy with incest or endogamy (marrying within the family), sometimes with a sister or brother (as in ancient Egypt) but more commonly with a more distant relative, such as a first cousin. It is thought that such marriages have a more solid foundation, and are more amenable to repair, since everyone within the family has an interest in smoothing things over, should problems arise either between the marriage partners or among the in-laws.[6] Another solution is to accept an outsider into the family as a marriage partner, but to cut her off from her family of birth. Then there is one in-law to contend with, but the power and influence reside within (usually the husband's) family, and the bride does not bring with her an entire assembly of in-laws. But most primitive societies, like our own, tolerate the tension between conjunction with and separation from the family which an in-law represents. The manner in which they deal with these problems, however, is very different from our own, yet surprisingly apt as a prevention of the annoyances we are expected to endure – which is why they may strike us as comical.

The two different but linked behaviours exhibited by many primitive societies towards in-laws are named by anthropologists 'strict avoidance' and 'compulsory joking'. The first involves behaviour which may appear rude – if a man's mother-in-law comes into a room in which he is present, he retreats to a corner and faces the wall until she leaves, or if he meets her on the open road, he retires into the bush – but it is really a form of respect, a means of preventing embarrassment and conflict. The bride may be permitted to visit and indeed receive visits from her parents, but still the contact must be between her and them, not between them and her husband. Should they stay the night while visiting her, they may be expected to sleep in a separate and distant hut, for some societies maintain a strong taboo against sleeping under the same roof as the child-in-law.

The companion practice, 'compulsory joking', is really the opposite to extreme respect. It is a relationship by which two people are by custom permitted, and in some instances required, to tease or make fun of one another. However extreme the teasing or abusive the language, neither party should take offence; etiquette is being followed, not broken, by such behaviour. This practice is sometimes interpreted as cathartic – it may be a way of ridding oneself of anger, or of preventing bad feelings from festering. But primarily it is a reminder of disjunction, in spite of the connection through marriage. It is practised towards younger siblings-in-law, or towards siblings-in-law of the same age, where the extreme respect of avoidance would be inappropriate. But both practices have the same end: the controlled acceptance and expression of in-law tension.

Problems among in-laws do not seem to be a function of personal incompatibility, of disapproval or of disagreement. The relationship itself is difficult. The earliest references to in-laws in the English language reveal this. The Oxford English Dictionary quotes a sixteenth-century remark that 'mothers in lawes beare a stepmothers hate unto their daughters in lawes'; in the seventeenth century, the reference is to the 'everlasting Din of Mothers-in-law'; and the eighteenth-century novelist Fielding acknowledges that 'the word mother-in-law has a terrible sound', while in the nineteenth century there appeared a comment in the *Daily Telegraph* that 'The drink of this name mother-in-law is composed of equal proportions of "old" and "bitter".' The despair over the relationship is as old as its name.

Some years ago a study of 500 married couples found that young, middle-class couples gave in-law trouble first place in their list of difficulties within the marriage.[7] At about the same time a study of working-class families in the East End of London showed how in-law tensions could influence the structure of a marriage.[8] Yet in general there has been a striking lack of research concerning in-law interaction. in the stereotypes derived from music-hall jokes and seaside postcards, it seems that the greatest tension is in regard to the mother-in-law, and this image was supported by my study: a woman is used to having power within the home. Her habitual domestic manner may well appear intrusive in someone else's home. But I found no age or class distinction, no reason to suppose that in-law problems are a function of immaturity of the younger couple – except in so far as many of us feel highly immature in regard to our in-laws. Differences in class and culture give rise to special kinds of in-law tension, but they do not account for the tension itself. This arises from the relationship itself, from the odd way in which in-laws reactivate former, crucial relationships and our fantasies connected with them. It arises from strange formations within the marriage bond itself, from profound sympathies and identification with the spouse, and from our fear of intimacy, which threatens our individuality. The story of in-law relationships is part of the story of marriage and parenthood, and it has been neglected for too long.

3
What Has Marriage Got to Do With In-Laws?

When we, as modern adults in Western society, decide to marry, we make our decision on the basis of our life-style, of our needs, of our affections – don't we? Our partner should be compatible with us, and our assessment of his or her character, and our assessment of our own emotions are what count. Neither property nor wealth nor social status are considered to be valid or holy issues in marriage. One accepts the other for better or for worse, for richer or for poorer, in sickness and in health. When a couple marry, they are acting on the assumption that they can live together in a way which will benefit them both. The assumption may be implausible, unrealistic or unwise, but the marriage would not go through without it.

When we marry we look to our adult identity, to opportunities to confirm and develop that identity. Our parents and siblings retain some hold upon our loyalty and love, but we

21

have separated ourselves from them and are better in touch with our adult selves than they. We know that, none the less, they may have firm ideas about which partner is good for us, and which bad, but surely that is their prejudice and their problem. Surely we ourselves leave our families of birth behind when we marry? Well, we often know that we don't, that our families are part of us and that therefore our spouse has his/her in-laws brought into the marriage by us, but we seldom understand how, and how extensively this is done.

Very roughly, we can consider three levels of marital choice. The first is social: someone is appropriate or acceptable on the basis of social class, education, religion, income, race. People vary greatly in the emphasis given to social compatibility. Some pride themselves on valuing it highly, believing, with a little justification, that marriages from within similar social groups have fewer problems. Some pride themselves on discarding social similarity, either because they believe love is above such considerations, or because they want to rebel against, or escape from, their social background.

The second level of choice is the one we think about and discuss most readily. This involves appreciation of the other's qualities – his or her physical attractiveness, character virtues, shared interests, ideals and ambitions. This is the conscious level of choice. We may feel in charge of these considerations, weighing up advantages and disadvantages to a match, choosing between one partner and another, deciding whether the time is ripe, whether to take the risk, whether to commit ourselves.

But deliberately adding up these pros and cons does not give us the sum on which we finally make our decision. We do not choose a marriage partner as we choose a friend, and a spouse is not simply a friend we happen to find attractive. While we are noticing how highly we regard someone, or how attractive we find someone, or how compatible we are or how comfortable we feel, we are dealing not only – and often not primarily – with qualities and characteristics we know we are thinking about. Our decisions are being formed and formulated by unconscious needs and desires. This is the third level

22

of marital choice. On this level we find the true rationale of marriage. In it we find explanations for the uncanny rightness of some choices, when the choice seems too quick, too unconsidered to everyone else. Also, we may find the justification for very bad marriages – for even bad choices have some rationale; the choice, however misguided, was made for some reason. Marital 'mistakes' are not like simple misreadings of a road map. They indicate either an incompatibility between our conscious and unconscious needs, or a need to be self-defeating, perhaps because one seeks punishment or because one needs an excuse to be exploited (as the only way of feeling needed). On this level we tend to 'know what we are doing' when we marry, though we seldom see what we are doing.

The pioneer marital therapist Henry Dicks said that there is 'strong evidence for viewing marital relations as the field of manifestation of unresolved earlier object relations par excellence: in many cases the *only* field'.[1] This means that people turn to their spouses to supply pleasures they obtained within earlier relationships and which they are reluctant to give up, or that they seek compensation for needs which were unmet in earlier relationships – almost always the issue is relationships with one's parents, or relationships which failed to develop with one's parents. The spouse's function is to supply what one lacked in one's family of birth, or to continue gratifying the needs that were met within one's family of birth. Marital relationships have as prototypes, or models, relationships with one's parents. Therefore the spouse finds herself or himself representing a father- or mother-in-law, and therefore, perhaps to his or her surprise, finds a stranger's identity thrust upon him.

A Fresh Start?

When people marry they do not break clean away from existing relations. In fact they have to make a profound double adjustment – to each other and to the relatives around them. They each to have reconcile their new obligation to their spouse with the old obligations and love for their parents.

23

This is a particularly 'hot' issue if the couple live with one partner's family, but even in a separate household the wife is aware of her husband's family of origin, and of her need to adjust to it, and he to hers. Any marital partner has been raised in a family, and in that family was given long and thorough training in implicit and explicit rules for dealing with people. The couple must reconcile long-term expectations based upon this training – and the matter is further confused by the fact that these expectations may run counter to conscious needs and expectations. A man who believes he values independence in his wife, but whose mother made a religion of caring for her home and family, may respond to his wife in the expectation that she will fulfil a traditional woman's role. Or a woman may have been raised in a family where there is an open show of emotion, and be confused by her husband's reserve. One partner may have been accustomed in his family to fierce but short-lived quarrels, whereas his wife may be terrified of quarrels – either because anger was considered taboo, or because quarrels led to severe disruption in her family – perhaps in the divorce of her parents. And there are hundreds of other issues which may require adjustment, or lead to irritation and conflict – such as the level or pitch of one's voice, the way one stands when one speaks to another person, the way one eats, the way one squeezes out the toothpaste. And in-laws are responsible for the spouse's training. They represent and support characteristics one may not like. Because they are a different family, they represent all that is strange and different and unwanted in the spouse. Because a spouse is not perfectly attuned to one's expectations, which developed within a different family of origin, the in-laws are guilty.

But is it not said that opposites attract, and that therefore we seek people whose families are different? Our marriage partner is our complement. We choose someone who has qualities, features or virtues which we lack. A domineering person will choose someone who is submissive, a person with little practical sense will choose someone who is obviously competent, a soft-hearted, sentimental person will choose someone who appears to put logic first. This trend is implicit in the reference to a spouse as 'my better half' – the spouse has what one does not, yet is also part of oneself. So the opposite is in the case of marriage not a matter of opposition but conjunction. And in order for this sense of belonging to arise within separation or difference, there has to be a good deal of symmetry too, where partners exchange the same sorts of behaviour – such as both giving to one another, both being sentimental, both being logical. Even if different roles are rigidly assigned within the marriage, so that one partner is always strong and the other always weak, there has to be some agreement as to how these roles are played out, or some agreement as to how situations and characteristics will be defined. So in order to complement one another as opposites there has to be an agreement (usually an unspoken and often unconscious one) as to what qualities are important. All people are alike and different in some ways. Which qualities are worthy of balancing? Which qualities that we lack are important to have in a spouse? What does being 'strong' mean? Is it being muscular or being decisive? Is a submissive complement to a domineering partner submissive only to the partner, or to everyone? People who see themselves as opposites usually agree on such things. They must therefore have a good deal in common.

In fact, the current, most prevalent theory among marital therapists as to why people marry is that people marry because they recognise in their partner a similar family background.[2] It is not that they swap stories about their childhoods and conclude that in important respects their families, and the development within their families, were the same. The recognition is much more immediate than that, and may be instantaneous, as when someone falls in love 'at first sight'. Information about a person's development is available at first sight – in his posture, in facial lines which indicate habitual expressions, in the way eye contact is made or avoided. Much more information becomes available on subsequent meetings, as certain things become accepted subjects of conversation and other topics are never mentioned –

perhaps the subject avoided is one's childhood. Moreover, people are quick to learn what level of emotional temperature is acceptable to another, which emotions are permitted expression, which emotions can be admitted only through mockery, and which must be denied.

The assumption behind this particular theory of attraction – that people marry someone who has similar childhood experiences – is that people choose as a partner someone who has got to the same stage of psychological development, or who has missed out at a similar stage. Perhaps, as an infant, our mother did not look after us adequately or was not sufficiently responsive – perhaps because she was depressed. Even in later childhood, the divorce of one's parents or the death of a parent may make a child feel rejected, and as an adult that person will tend to choose someone who also felt rejected or abandoned as a child. It is generally believed that the earlier the stage at which one has missed out, the more severe the developmental arrest is. Someone who has not had adequate mothering will be very bad at forming any close relationship – yet there might be the following success story: one person may use the marriage, and seek in the partner, a substitute for inadequate parenting, while the partner, having also missed out in an early, intense stage of being mothered, may be glad to see someone try to bring out love in him/her. Or one partner may need someone who cannot give too much love – perhaps because she/he is anxiously attached to a previous relationship. This may happen if the relationship was both crucial and unsatisfactory. It may have failed to give one the confidence and trust to develop further, and yet one is attached to it because it is the only attachment one knows (hence the term 'anxiously attached'), and one cannot let go of the hope that something will come of it. Therefore one seeks a spouse who will not demand 'disloyalty' to the previous attachment, someone who in fact will not demand much love, because he/she for a similar reason cannot offer love.

There are many stages of development, and many stages at which one can suffer developmental arrest. It may be when we are learning to separate from our parents, or to share our

26

parents' love with others, or to accept challenge, criticism and teasing from our siblings or friends. If we guard ourselves from the things we should have learned during these stages, we will probably choose someone who also must be protected from them, and who therefore does not admit to them and in that way protects us from them too. Or, at the stage during which we first express anger and see the affect of our anger on the parents, we may discover that our parents cannot handle this anger, cannot reassure us that they will not be destroyed by it. Therefore we come to fear anger, and try to suppress it, and would choose someone who would deny anger too, because we have not learned to accept our own and are afraid of its effect.

We tend to choose a partner with the same kinds of emotion 'behind the screen' – but the particular techniques of defending against those emotions and fears (and shame at those fears and defences) might be very different. Indeed, they might be opposite and complementary, making it look as though opposites attract, though it is in reality similarity that attracts. Or perhaps we have had to cope with some sadness, some disappointment, and we defend ourselves against it by being superstrong, whereas another person defends him/herself against it by being dependent and weak. We will pick out a certain type of strength, or a certain type of dependence, as being significantly opposite to us because it is directed towards the same need.

Expectation and Betrayal

If we look at our choice of partner in this way, we will have a better understanding of why it is that our in-laws' peculiarities irritate or even enrage us. As adults we all have some capacity for tolerating differences in people. Some of us are very good at it. But few of us are good at tolerating our in-laws' differences. Their assumptions about how we should conduct our lives or handle our domestic arrangements may be intrusive, but even if our in-laws are tactful and reserved, they annoy us. The quickness with which our hostility is aroused may indeed be linked to our desire to construct a family like our family of origin, to reproduce its emotional atmosphere, in which certain feelings were acceptable and certain feelings were taboo, in which certain defences worked well and others were unnecessary, in which we may be protected from challenge in many areas, in which sympathy will be automatic, because our partner focuses on similar fears and similar needs. Even when we believe we have married the unexpected, when our partner, after marriage, seems full of surprises, the patterns which appear in marriage usually existed before the ceremony. Even when we appear to be self-defeating we have usually been pretty careful to choose what we want or what we think we deserve, or what we are used to – for even abuse may feel 'right' to us. We are choosing someone who may be the worst possible choice, since he/she shares with us our impediments and limitations, and therefore may prevent us from developing, yet we have chosen someone who may also be a good choice because he/she shares our needs and understands our fears, and is the best possible person to help us grow and adapt.

We have chosen a person on the basis of similar family history. And yet we discover every time we meet them that our in-laws are different from our own family. The irritation or rage we feel signals a sense of betrayal. 'This is not my family!', we protest. 'This is nothing like my family. I do not see my family in these strangers.'

We may feel we have been cheated. We may feel we have made the wrong choice. We wanted to reproduce our own family, not the family which these strangers produced. Yet what we based our choice on, usually, was the partner him/herself, and the significant similarities involved the partner's response to his/her family and to the problems and pleasures which arose during his/her development, and all this may be very different from our response to another person's family. So we have a collision not only between different families meeting within marriage, or as a result of marriage, but a collision of different families in conjunction with the (usually unconscious) expectation that they be the same.

And what about the parents-in-law? They are people, too, and like all people feel comfortable with some children-in-law and uncomfortable with others. The parents-in-law, too, make assumptions about what similarities are significant and should be preserved within the family, and the extent to which differences are allowed. After all, the ideal parent-in-law to child-in-law relationship is to forget about the 'in-law' tag, to see the child-in-law as a son or daughter. Yet children-in-law put parents-in-law on the defensive. They threaten not merely loyalty and affection by suddenly becoming the primary person in their child's life, but also the cultural values they have worked so hard to instil in their children. Also, the child-in-law signals the parent's declining power; the spouse's influence is now paramount.

Sometimes parents-in-law try to overcome this threat by idealising their son- or daughter-in-law. By assuming that the in-law is 'good', they are protecting themselves from the fear that someone over whom they may have no control has the power to make or break their child's life. I will never forget the way my mother-in-law pronounced my first brother-in-law's name. 'Anthony', she would say, with the rhythm of butter spreading on warm toast. He gave her nothing of himself (this is usually called 'keeping a low profile') and so she constructed something that was a cross between God and a seven-year-old child helping out in the kitchen. Any conflict within the marriage was assumed to be her daughter's fault. After all, she had some influence over her, and had a fighting chance of placating her, and persuading her to placate her husband, whereas even then she must have suspected possible dangers in the husband. The angelic image was shattered by her son-in-law's infidelity, but even then my mother-in-law hoped that, if her daughter would only curb her temper and make an effort, things would come right in the end. The parents-in-law may side with the child-in-law because that is, in their view, the best way of smoothing over an argument. If the child-in-law is good, then the parent-in-law has a chance of controlling the marriage, because he/she has some control of the child. Many people say their parents always take their spouse's side in a quarrel. The parents-in-law's idealisation of the child-in-law may well be infuriating because it casts him/her in a certain role (I will have more to say about this common problem later) and because the child-in-law is aware that it is either an attempt to deny the strangeness the parents-in-law know to be lurking in him/her or an indication of a wish to stabilise (therefore interfere with) the marriage.

When a child-in-law does harm one's child, the parent usually suffers despair and anger. For the cruellest child-in-law is cruel to one's own child, not to oneself. This is the genuine fear behind much of the parent-in-law's carping. For the cruel spouse is cruel to one's child not as a member of the family may be cruel. A spouse, unlike a parent, is seldom 'cruel to be kind'. A spouse does not spar with one's child as does a brother or sister. A spouse's cruelty is seen as a stranger's cruelty.

Do We Marry Our Parents?

It is clear that the marriage itself is bound in many ways with the parental home. The relationship between any husband and wife bears a close and complex relationship to the parent–child history. The platitude that emerged in the 1950s, with the popularisation of Freud's work on the Oedipus complex, is that men marry their mothers and women marry their fathers – or try to. The theory behind the platitude is that a boy, at about the age of four or five, comes to see his mother as sexually desirable. As a result, he hates his father as a rival, but also looks up to him and tries to identify with him, because the father possesses sexually the woman he desires but cannot have, because he lacks the genital equipment at that stage and, more importantly, because his father would punish him in some awful way (Freud thought the primary fear at this stage was the fear of castration – a punishment fitting to the crime). Therefore, to protect himself, the child must suppress his romantic love for his mother, make do with being as much like the father as possible and then, as an adult, choose a woman who represents, or is similar to, the mother.

The story of the girl's romantic attachment was thought to have a similar outcome, though it was somewhat more complicated because her first romantic attachment, too, was to the mother, whom she rejected only upon discovering that the woman lacked a penis, was therefore deformed and had passed on this deformity to her. The young girl, suffering shame, disgust and rage, turns to her father, who alone can give her, by proxy, a penis which she sees as necessary to anatomical completion. She, too, cannot fulfil this desire by having intercourse with her father, for she still has some love and loyalty to her mother. So she identifies with her mother, whose shame is somewhat modified by sexual possession of the father. The girl becomes as much like her mother as possible, and chooses a marriage partner who is modelled on, or even in fact represents, her father, her first male romance figure.

Well, people sometimes do search for their fathers and mothers in a spouse. They may end up hating one another for not being the parent – as Martha despises George in Edward Albee's play *Who's Afraid of Virginia Woolf?*. Martha thought her father was a brilliant man. He *was* the history department, whereas George is a disappointment to her because he is merely *in* the history department. We find many real-life counterparts of marital disappointment based on parental contrasts. While working on a previous book I interviewed a woman who described her husband as the greatest impediment to her career, and said that he found her work as a university professor sterile because it was not creative, like his mother's work, which was of a more traditional, home-making type. Her husband's image of what she should be continued to intrude upon her self-respect, and her husband thought she should do a different type of work because his mother, who remained his female ideal, had done it.

But problems about career goals and achievements are not the most crucial problems to arise from the attempt to marry one's parent or the desire to see one's marriage partner as one's parent. The suppression of romantic desires for one's parent during the Oedipal stage, after all, was necessary because one felt guilty about these desires. If one sees a spouse as a parent, then the satisfaction of sexual desire for the parent/spouse will arouse tremendous guilt and anxiety. One feels one should not be sleeping with this person, or one should not desire this person, because one sees the partner as the parent. Sometimes this identification can emerge long after the marriage ceremony. The birth of a child may trigger it, or the death of a parent may persuade one to seek his/her embodiment in the spouse.

Christopher lost all desire for his wife when his son was born. Pat was now a mother, and represented his mother. Or perhaps he so identified and empathised with his new son that he saw his wife as the son did, as a woman towards whom sexual feelings were prohibited. In any case, he felt the need to seek many other women out as sexual partners, while denying any sexuality in his wife. This case is one among the many in which the mother image is sanctified, and removed from the sexual arena, to protect oneself against the confusion between mother and lover.

People do seek out their mother or father in a spouse, but this is not the rule, nor is it the normal pattern. Rather, it is gross simplification or caricature of the normal pattern, in which we seek in a partner what we valued in our parents – both in our mother and father. Admiration is not limited to the parent of our own sex, and ideal partners are constructed from qualities found – or wanting – in both parents.

We, at our best, employ the ability to form attachments which we learned as dependent children, but seek an attachment that will encourage and support our adult identity. We appreciate our partner for his or her likeness to our family, for sharing rules about what can and cannot be expressed, sharing emotional needs and psychological aims, yet also we appreciate him/her for not being a parent or a brother or sister, for being different – perhaps startlingly different and making up for what our family lacked.

But of course we are not always at our best, and it is easy to confuse parental love with marital love: the people closest to us may add to the confusion.

Parents know, on some level, that their child is working with an internalised model of them and the family life they have created when he/she chooses a spouse. Generally parents feel this should be so, and generally they judge the spouse according to their self-image or their family ideal – for they may have little contact with the model their child actually derived from them. The frequent complaint, either spoken or implied, that someone is 'not good enough' for their child, is an assessment not only of their child's worth but also of the value of the models they believe they have instilled in their child. So the question becomes not only, 'Is this person good enough to marry my child?' but also, 'Is this person good enough to represent me?'

Marriage is a balance between family and outsider. It is a balance between self-identity and one's complement. This is not an easy balance to maintain. It may well be more difficult for the in-laws than for the spouse, since the in-laws seldom share the positive emotions which presumably motivated the choice of the spouse. Parents, when they look at a child-in-law, face their child's image of themselves, or their child's image of what they need but lack. It is no wonder, then, that a son- or daughter-in-law may insult or shock the parent-in-law without knowing why, and with the parent-in-law offering the most petty and prejudicial excuses. Mirror images often do that to us.

Sibling Rivalry

Since our attraction to other people, and our choice of a marital partner, are developed in and closely bound up with our family of birth, it is likely that there will be cross attractions between brothers-in-law and sisters-in-law – not only between one's brother and one's wife, but even between one's wife and one's sister's husband. Our brothers and sisters were raised in the same family, and though of course their history is none the less different from ours – because they have different needs, different responses and were perhaps treated differently – there are enough points of similarity to expect some similarity

33

of marital choice. And because we tend to choose people who help us reproduce our families of birth, or who help us provide what we lacked in our families, choosing a spouse who can do this because he/she missed out, or got stuck on, the same stage of development, then the people we choose and the people our sisters or brothers choose may well have good reason to be attracted to one another. And of course all this cross attraction does not pave the way for good and simple friendships, but for the defence, jealousy and annoyance we suffer when we look at someone else's image of us or of someone with whom we identify.

When my brother-in-law first met me he commented to my husband (his wife's brother) that he liked me but thought I would be 'quite a handful'. This remark, which perhaps should not be interpreted too literally (did he imagine handling me, and then reject the idea?) reveals a typical pattern of a response to a sibling-in-law. There is appreciation, which often sounds little more than polite, and then a modification, or criticism, which asserts that the brother- or sister-in-law would not have been their choice. 'She's not bad looking, a bit too tough. Takes herself too seriously', Cathy's husband remarked about his brother's fiancée, and Cathy admitted that she was relieved, because her brother-in-law's fiancée had indeed not only been good looking, but, in her opinion, 'had the looks my husband goes for'.

Another woman said that she had not given her new sister-in-law another thought, until her husband started criticising her.

He kept saying he would never marry a woman like that, and what must his brother think when other men looked at her, and wouldn't he change his tune about liking an independent wife when they had children. I think my husband believes that if he'd waited a little longer to marry, or had been a little younger himself, he would have chosen a different type of woman – a more modern version, you know. I don't really think it would suit him, but he may feel cheated because he didn't even think of trying. The big

34

wave of the feminist movement – I mean when it stopped being embarrassing – came just a little too late for him.

This woman understood the major focus of such criticisms of siblings-in-law. The spouse may well be reassured by such criticism, but the real point is to defend oneself against possible attraction, or against the sense that one's brother, sister, brother-in-law or sister-in-law have done better than oneself. We always feel better if we convince ourselves that the options we took are the options we would still take, given the chance to choose again, or given a wider range of choice. It is not easy to live with regrets, or with anxiety as to whether we should regret our choice. And our siblings, and even our siblings-in-law, who become part of our close peer group, show us what might have been possible for us, what might have been different, and maybe better. Did we balance our needs properly, or did our sibling do a better job? We may identify so closely with our sibling that we feel his/her needs are ours, and that we should have met our needs in precisely the same way. Also, as a legacy of sibling rivalry, remains the niggling insistence, no matter how much we care for their well-being, to assess ourselves as better off than they. Often the husband and wife collude with one another in this, dismissing a brother- or sister-in-law, or a brother- or sister-in-law's spouse, in order to defend themselves against self-dissatisfaction. Sometimes a brother- or sister-in-law is not seen (avoided) for years, or a particularly successful one is described as 'snooty' or, with greater sophistication but the same result, 'narcissistic'. I found that often a person was not particularly proud of his/her more famous sibling, and that the spouse supported his/her negative views. Not only did people want to defend themselves against cross attraction to siblings-in-law, but also against envy of the sibling, and the spouses were highly cooperative in this – possibly because in this way they defended themselves against cross attraction to their sibling-in-law.

But people do not always have to limit their appreciation of others in order to be at peace with themselves. Often we enjoy siblings-in-law for the same reasons we enjoy siblings – they are people good at understanding us because they are roughly using the same defences or overcoming the same fears, because they have missed out on or become stuck at a similar stage of development, or because they are different people, yet belong to the same family. In such cases we may get pleasure from the very things others have to defend themselves against – the cross attractions, the sense that siblings and siblings-in-law suggest how our own lives might have been different, and we are able to extend our identity through that of others, rather than feel threatened. When my second brother-in-law (my sister-in-law's second husband) and I first met, he now reports thinking, 'Well anyone with a sister-in-law who wears shoes like that can't be a bad match.' This is a humorous embrace of the feeling that if he finds something attractive in the other woman in the family (even if the best thing about her is her expensive shoes!) then the family is probably the right one for him.

But of course brothers- and sisters-in-law are not always attracted to one another, not even unconsciously, and this lack of attraction within families often leads to distaste (it may be low-grade distaste or actual revulsion). Who is this stranger usurping the attention of our sister? we may think. Perhaps we enjoyed a very close relationship with our sibling, and are reluctant to share his/her company, or, indeed, his/her love and loyalty. We often do have romantic feelings towards a sibling, especially one of the opposite sex, and this may emerge in jealousy when our sibling marries, or in a continuing effort after the marriage to denigrate or minimise the significance of the marital tie, as opposed to the natural blood bond between brother and sister. Sometimes a jealous brother or sister will do everything in his/her power to prevent a marriage. Each possible partner has something wrong with him/her and the sibling will think the objections are directed towards the partner, but they are really aimed against marriage itself. This type of jealousy may well be linked to the transfer of power and money to the sibling's spouse – certainly this particular type of jealousy is more common in powerful and wealthy families. In the prominent Chandler family of Pasadena, Norman's sisters disapproved of every potential mate for their brother, and it took Dorothy Buffum, from an ambitious Long Beach family, to fight her way through their criticisms, to gain Norman's commitment in marriage and to retain her influence during the marriage. The Chandler women were perhaps jealous not only of their handsome brother but also of the family name, with its weight and wealth, that would pass to their sister-in-law's children rather than to their children.

Property and wealth, its transfer and inheritance, often complicate in-law relationships, but they are usually the excuse not the cause of in-law problems. Among working-class families in England, too, quarrels with one's siblings-in-law are frequent; and when they do occur they are most likely to be, as in the Chandler family, between the wife and her husband's siblings. Reasons given for conflicts – even conflicts which lead to long-term alienation – are slight. Someone has said something that could be interpreted as an insult, someone believes her brother-in-law 'thinks too much of himself', someone thinks her sister-in-law 'is always criticising her'. But the real motive for conflict is a wife's desire to make sure the husband's loyalties are on her side, or the need to define her family as the dominant one. Husbands sometimes, too, seek to minimise the influence of a sister- or brother-in-law on the wife, but usually this is done more rationally, by speaking to the wife, criticising her sibling to her, rather than quarrelling with a sibling-in-law and refusing to see him/her again. This more subtle method may also be more effective, for when a person's siblings are banned from the marital home, visits tend to continue, but in the sibling's home, and without one's spouse. In this way the sibling might have more influence, and even if the spouse is never mentioned, her/his absence will be telling, and she/he may appear as a defeated spectre – defeated because, after all, the visit between the siblings is taking place. Quarrels among in-laws seldom have a final line. Banishment or expulsion do not end them. They continue as long as the marriage.

Can We Avoid Having In-Laws?

Marriage gives one in-laws. Do couples who live together and share their lives, their property and their children without undergoing a marriage ceremony have an easier, less in-law like time with their partner's family?

The answer is 'no'. Since issues underlying in-law problems are loyalty, the sharing of love and affection, the difficulty in seeing people outside one's family as intimate with a member of one's family, they arise with any union between one's family member and an outsider, whether or not that union is legally binding, whether or not there are proper in-laws. Moreover, such unmarried couples almost invariably face an additional problem with their partner's family – that of not being married. 'Where does that leave my child?' the parents worry. 'Why is this outsider refusing to offer my child the official sanction of marriage?' or, if the reluctance to marry is seen to be on one's child's part, 'Why is my child wasting his/her time with someone who is not suitable for marriage?'

To many parents, the absence of a marriage ceremony is such a sore point that they ignore or deny the intimacy between their child and his/her partner. The couple may be living together, but when they visit the parental homes they are given separate rooms, and their separation is enforced by the partner's mother carrying out the intrusive English custom of delivering early morning tea to the bedside. This custom does not end with marriage, and the constraint it puts upon a couple is obvious, and has been neatly documented by a cartoonist[3] as the brisk entry which interrupts intercourse and which is not embarrassing because the mother-in-law simply does not see what is going on. But if sexuality is denied during marriage, it is more vehemently and insultingly denied before marriage.

In-laws tend to have trouble doing anything right, or their in-laws take exception to whatever they do, because the instances in which a parent-in-law does not behave like this, and behaves in the opposite way, offend just as easily. When one woman's mother brought her tea in the morning, she looked around the room in amazement and said, 'Where's Frank?'

A partner's parents find it difficult to ignore the question of marriage. The relationship never seems settled to them until a ceremony occurs. Some parents come out boldly with the question, 'Are you going to marry my daughter, then?', but more often they practise a formalised politeness and tend to question their own child in private. It is very difficult for the couple not to feel pressured in such conditions, and this pressure tends to make at least one of them (usually the child's partner, who has no relationship with the parents other than as child's partner) a cipher, a receptacle for doubt and disappointment.

The parents who exert this type of pressure may make themselves ridiculous, but they none the less are often effective, sometimes more with their child's partner than with their own child. In one instance a young woman's parents were French, bound to the libertarian principles of the 1960s, and did not wish their daughter to marry, presenting many arguments against it: would not children of the union be happier thinking that their parents stayed together because they wanted to, rather than because they were bound by law? What kind of irrational law forced one to promise to love someone always, when it was well known that such a promise simply could not be kept, and was tantamount to asking someone to promise to pretend to love another in order to find social acceptance for one's present love? Marriage involved conspiracy with hypocrisy, and the honest person would prefer an anomalous but honourable marriageless union. Yvette's boyfriend, on the other hand, came from a lower-middle-class Scottish family, in which living together without being married was quite simply 'living in sin'. The couple, being based in Britain, were closer to the disapproving scrutiny of the boyfriend's parents – perhaps this was their trump. For the woman eventually suggested to her boyfriend that they marry, and they did. Her parents-in-law were delighted, helped organise the wedding, and proferred many gifts. Yvette's parents remained in France, and made no acknowledgement of the ceremony.

A few years later, when the marriage was breaking up, Alasdair challenged his wife, 'Why, when you were so disapproving of marriage and everything to do with the marital institution, did you turn around and suggest we get married?' Her reply was that she had wanted to please his parents.

Was this just a swipe at him? No, because she was not saying she had not loved him or that she had not truly wanted to live with him, but only that she had decided to marry him in order to please his parents.

But why should the parent-in-law's approval matter? Why should young people who are independent and apparently secure in one another's affection cater to the desires of the parent-in-law? Is this a legacy of that self-defeating need to please others, which many girls, in particular, develop at an early age, even in the care of determinedly liberated parents? For whereas young men, too, marry under pressure, it is usually under pressure of their partner, or the pressure of their own parents. Do women, on the other hand, feel more pressure to sustain other's image of them as family-makers, or have they a greater need to be part of a family, to view themselves in relation to others, and to ensure that others are comfortable with them? I think this is so, but the problem is not simply one of failed spirit, or failed independence.

Because we are uncertain about what our parents-in-law think of us, and because we usually feel that they do not like us as much as either they or we think they should, any self-doubt we may have is aggravated in relation to them. If we sometimes feel awkward, we will certainly feel awkward – or ugly, or silly, or outrageous – in their presence. We may go to enormous and uncharacteristic lengths to please them – for the very reasons we may go to great lengths to displease them. We try to please them, or we try to shock them, just to learn where we stand with them. Yvette's discomfort at Alasdair's parents' disapproval was such that she was willing to relinquish her independent, unmarried status.

By choosing a partner we hope to complete, or reproduce, or perhaps compensate for, our own family. And these hopes, as we shall see, can create sharp conflict with our needs to develop individually and autonomously. In regard to our partner we may relinquish some independence and individuality for the better – this is part of intimacy, and intimacy is certainly necessary to human well-being. In regard to our parents-in-law, however, we feel we relinquish part of ourselves for the worse, out of weakness, out of a desire to please. The outcome of such bargains is frustration, disappointment and anger.

41

4
My Spouse, My Self

When John came upstairs on Sunday night, Megan knew something was wrong, and she knew why. Her mother-in-law, a widow, always telephoned at eight o'clock on Sunday. 'It puts the rest of the evening all out of focus', she remarked. This call was particularly upsetting because his mother had announced that she was due to visit them – 'It's been some time since I've seen the children' – and the only week she could manage was the week before Easter. She had it all planned – when she would arrive, when she would leave. Megan knew that her husband had just negotiated with his business partner to take that week off so that the family might go away on holiday – the children had a long spring holiday, which Megan knew she would find wearing. Megan also knew that John would not have explained this to his mother, but would have said, 'Yes, that's fine', and then been in a bad temper about it. 'He's thirty-seven years old. Isn't it time he got his mother out of his hair? I wish I could tell him to sort her out.'

This couple seemed to be at odds, yet their tactics were very similar. John could not bring himself to explain to his mother that the week she proposed to visit was not convenient – which would be a totally reasonable thing to do – and Megan could not bring herself to remind her husband of this, and to insist upon her right to take their planned holiday, which would also be reasonable enough. Nor did she think of taking on her mother-in-law herself, and explaining that the family had made other plans. Both were paralysed in face of the mother-in-law's decision to visit, both were angry, and each took out this anger on the other.

Megan was angry because her husband was putting her second – a common enough complaint *vis-à-vis* the mother-in-law – but she was also angry on her husband's behalf. His mother had put him out as much as her. Why did he let her do that? Why was he not better equipped to defend himself? Why did he allow his mother's whim to make him unhappy?

With Whom Are We Angry?

Sometimes our complaints against our parents-in-law are really about the effect our parents-in-law have on our spouse. After all, many people behave differently with their parents. They may regress. Forgotten dependencies emerge, as do former fears and loyalties. Parents may stimulate unusual behaviour because they have an outdated image of their child, or because their image was inappropriate. Yet children – and even adults capable of leading independent lives are the children of their parents – usually respond to their parents' image of them, even when they know it is wrong. The parent's image of the child represents, at least to the child, what the parent needs the child to be. It is difficult to underestimate how thoroughly people adopt their parents' expectations and wishes as their own, even to the extent of failing in order to make their parents' more accepting of their own lives, or of being a 'problem' in order to remove the focus from the parents' other (often marital) problems. But of course a parent's wishes do not always exert a self-defeating control upon us. We may respond to only minor expectations – such as what type of language is permissible, or how our own children should behave, or how self-assertive we should be. As adults, our parents' expectations may work upon us only in their presence. Basically we are free of them, but there are echoes, which sound loudly at certain times. We may not hear them, but our spouse is probably a keener listener than anyone else.

So we may be complaining about our in-laws, when our real anger is with our spouse. One mother-in-law noticed this. She said that when her son made much of her, her daughter-in-law would get 'sharp' or 'catty'. Yet the issue is not always jealousy, not simply a question of who comes first or who is best loved. Often the battle is about what we think people should be, what we judge to be best for them, and what we think will make them happy. Parents and spouses may well have different notions about these things, and these differences will then become battlegrounds.

What we are fighting for, and what we are fighting about, is not always clear. It is not only the story of our marital choice, but also the story of what goes on within our marriage that is based upon previous development. Many problems between marriage partners develop as a result of their identification of the other as a parent. One man and woman were having difficulty in their marriage, and consulted a marital therapist. The man repeatedly referred back to the time his parents had been killed in an air raid. His wife sought to comfort him with embraces and love-making. He was shocked by her approach. What he needed, he claimed, was to talk about his feelings. He believed that physical contact, and sexual pleasure, would be an affront to his parents. This is an understandable position – there is no reason we should feel that sexual intimacy is always all right – but it is not simple or straightforward. It emerged in therapy that the man always wanted to 'talk things out', that he wanted to intellectualise his feelings in order to keep his wife at a distance, and he wanted to keep her at a distance because she was a mother-substitute (and therefore physical intimacy was linked to guilt); but also he wanted to keep her at a distance because he did not want to be like his father, whom he considered to be over-intrusive and over-emotional.[1] It is very common for us to resist identification with a parent by being deliberately different – but we do this when we already feel the pressure of identification, when we believe already that we are similar. The wife therefore was part of her parents-in-law's history, and unwittingly was both subject and actor in their drama.

Such configurations of feelings and images from the past are part of all marriages. Indeed, marriage seems to be the central adult stage for the reenactment of our first relationships and our development through normal stages, or of abnormal impediments in these relationships. And so, to understand what is going on in marriage, and with our parents and our parents-in-law, we should understand something of how we develop as people who need and respond to others.

The Story So Far . . .

We can only give an approximate account of what is going on in the infant's mind. The theory that makes the most sense of personality development as a whole gets its starting-point from the fact that, because of the physical weakness and helplessness of the human infant, survival depends upon that kind of devoted care we call mothering. It is not known at what stage the baby becomes aware of this, though it occurs early – within the first few weeks of life. This can be seen from the particular alertness and activity of the baby when the mother's face is visible or her voice is audible. The earliest emotional life is concentrated on this relationship. Through it the baby first experiences itself and its world. Is the human world the baby is getting to know a kind one? Is there any basis for trust, for confidence? Will fear or discomfort be soothed, or will one be hammered by them until one has lost the capacity for feeling?

The baby's awareness of his helplessness complicates the dependence. For what is involved is not only a physical dependence but repeated proof that the dependence will work,

46

continuous assurance that someone is responding to the baby. If the child's needs are not met quickly and accurately, he may suffer anger and despair that verges on panic. Any parent knows what this sounds like, and all parents have to make their child endure it. Perhaps the baby cannot be fed or held just at that minute. Perhaps nothing will waylay the baby's boredom as the caretaker waits at the check-out counter, or is stuck in a traffic jam. Perhaps the earache or stomach pain will not subside. When panic takes over, the baby feels something like disintegration or annihilation. The baby's cries at this stage elicit a strong response from any normal person. Even very young children will try to soothe a baby – or will cover their ears to protect themselves from the infectious panic. An adult will tend to hold the baby – and this is reassuring. It seems to give back to the baby a sense of wholeness and security.

Yet the baby cannot avoid discomfort completely, and, it is thought, develops two specific psychological techniques of dealing with it. First, the baby imagines him- or herself as being comfortable or satisfied, or imagines having what would be satisfying. A hungry baby will imagine that he or she is sucking. A baby in pain will imagine thrusting off the complaint like a blanket. When this is not successful, the baby eliminates discomfort by a particular method of denial: the discomfort – the pain or hunger or boredom or frustration – does not belong to the baby but to something or someone else. This method of denial is the basis of projection, and it is used throughout our lives to cope with pain, disappointment, anger and failure. We are not angry, but someone else is attacking us. We did our best, but someone else failed us, did not make the proper effort, the correct decision. We have not been hurt by a quarrel, but are pleased to think that the break-up of the friendship will be the other's loss.

The infant, however, is more or less stuck with the caretaker. He or she can project anger and pain onto the parent, so that the parent who frustrates the baby and makes him angry is the cruel, selfish, destructive stepmother of fairy tales. But the infant still needs a loving, mothering person. The infant cannot completely reject the parent. So what does he or she do? How does he or she preserve the attachment to the person who constantly smiles, who is full of admiration for him or her, who fondles and feeds the child? It is thought that at a very early stage the baby splits the good from the bad. Perhaps the baby projects the bad qualities of the mother – her inability to heal every pain immediately, her refusal to pick him or her up at a particular moment, her abandonment of the child in his cot – onto someone or something else, or perhaps he or she sees the mother as two people – the good mother and the bad mother. Or, of course, the infant may project the good mother or her good qualities onto someone or something else, and see her as bad. The child goes through various stages of conflict and ambivalence. One of the most important tasks of the growing child is to learn to integrate the good and bad in the mother and the good and bad in himself. The people closest to the child can help by showing that they are not destroyed by his anger, and that therefore that anger is not something which will destroy the good part of his or her world, that it is something which can be tolerated, that it may disappear as quickly as it came, that it is outweighed by love.

The infant's initial total dependence on the mother – the stage during which he or she seems to face annihilation or disintegration when his or her needs are not promptly met – usually ends at about a year. Then the baby is – at certain moments, for a certain period of time, with certain people, in certain relationships – what we can think of as a whole person. The baby has some self boundary, some sense that there is an edge to himself or herself. The child is still dependent upon the mother's protection from too much stimulation – either excitement or fear – which cannot be processed; but, on the other hand, the child needs some stimulation and some frustration to develop awareness of being separate and different – in particular from the mother.

As the child becomes more mobile, and experiences the euphoria of mastering physical skills, the awareness of separation may become so intense that he or she retreats to the mother and clings to her. The unmistakable symptoms of the 'terrible twos' grow from a desire both to hurt and to control. The child feels the need to control the mother because he/she cannot control anger and frustration, and is afraid that bad feelings will alienate her – as angry as he or she may be with her, because she is imperfect, the child needs the mother, and therefore must keep her and must have power over her. Also, the child may become incredibly confused by the parents' projections onto him or her, just as he or she is learning about the difference between him/herself and them. All parents project onto their children hopes and fears and wishes, and no child is ever fully able to separate himself or herself from these projections. They form part of the child's identity.

In the second year of life the child's gender identity is formed – the child sees itself clearly as either a boy or a girl, even though he/she may not understand all the implications of gender. From this identity emerges what is widely known as the Oedipal complex, though this is rarely as straightforward as has been classically presented. The boy does not love the mother and hate the father. The girl does not hate the mother and love the father. Most generally and fairly the Oedipal situation can be described as the child's realisation that though he or she is attached both to the mother and the father, and though they both love him/her and though he/she has a claim on them, they have a relationship with one another from which he/she is excluded. The two people who matter most to him/her have a bond to one another which he/she cannot understand, but which he/she senses is totally different from any relationship he/she can have with either of them. The child does not turn towards one parent and away from the other. It is a triangular situation whereby the child remains attached to both parents, but feels the pull towards one – the parent of the opposite sex – and is jealous of the same-sexed parent, but also worries that he/she is betraying the other parent, and at the same time feels betrayed by the parents' sexual relationship.

The crucial psychological skills to be learned from this stage are, first, the ability to share people with one another, to allow them a wider emotional life than they have with oneself; and the second skill is to tolerate simultaneous and intense loving and hating. The girl knows that she loves her mother, but she also has new strong feelings for her father which make her want to rival her mother. The boy loves and is devoted to his father, even though he wishes he could have his mother all to himself, and hates the father as an intruder. Love, hate, rivalry, jealousy, puzzlement are all part of this stage when the child's love of and identification with his/her parents make him/her both want to be like each parent and also to be complementary to both.

Marriage and Infancy

Many of the patterns of unconscious longings and fears that are part of the unwritten – and often unacknowledged – marriage contract are derived from these infantile and child-hood relationships. What do we expect from marriage? How much do we expect from it? What will one's partner do for one? What will one be to one's partner? We find the reasons behind these expectations in past relationships. Sometimes we feel compelled, unconsciously, to repeat patterns formed by our parents. Sometimes we do our best to avoid, we think, the patterns of our parents' marriage or of our relationship with our parents, yet we manage to repeat them perfectly, some unseen will guiding us and undermining all conscious decisions and determinations. Our spouse inherits his or her parents-in-law's marriage, the parents-in-law's history of relationships with their children.

Time and time again the people who spoke to me about their in-laws apologised for being so petty – they felt they were irritated by small faults, by inconsequential habits, yet the irritation drove them to tears. The fact is that their complaints were profound and crucial. They were irritated by the burden of their inheritance. They were asked to melt away bad feelings their parents-in-law had given their spouse. They were asked for continual reassurance on points which meant nothing to them. Why did the wife need to be told over and

50

over again that she was loved, or that she was a competent mother, or that she was not a typical mother? Why did the husband need to prove that he was not a 'stick in the mud', or that he was a strong man, completely in control of the baby in himself? Why did he expect to be treated like a king, and why did he find housework demeaning? These patterns and characteristics may have emerged in the marriage and yet have gone against all conscious beliefs and expectations of the person who exhibits them. The mature aims of the marriage can be undermined by repressed or unconscious emotions, or by rigid internal patterns. The parents-in-law do indeed play a large part in the marriage.

But sometimes the partners can snap out of old patterns quite suddenly, seeing the humour of the confused identifications. One man, who feared that he was like his overbearing father, was beginning to act more and more like his father. He would dictate the family's schedule-making plans for each family member from breakfast time until bedtime. He arranged all the details of his daughter's car pool, even though it was his wife who drove it. He issued instructions on shopping, the preparation of meals, the behaviour which was acceptable at mealtime, and the conversations which were deemed appropriate. At first his wife thought that he was being helpful – or trying to be helpful – in this domestic participation, but he began to treat all other family members as though their thoughts were too insignificant to be considered. Finally his wife stood her ground, defending herself and her children, and giving him a good dressing down. He stared at her in amazement, and then burst into laughter. He had been feeling like his father, and feeling trapped into overbearingness because he had an indecisive wife – as indeed his father had had. He had felt compelled to take charge because he had been seeing his wife as his mother, and he knew how to take charge only as his father had taken charge, with control over petty details, with an arrogant dismissal of others' ideas. When his wife stood up to him he was exuberant because he saw that she was unlike his mother, and would prevent him from becoming like his father.

The Marital Dyad

An important element is missing from the previous descriptions of marital disappointment and conflict, and the parents' or parents-in-law's part in it, and that is the way in which the partners themselves agree on what they will argue about, and what turn their arguments will take, and who will be upset about what, and by how much. The couple work as a team to construct tolerable problems and avoid intolerable ones. Of course this teamwork can get out of hand; the intolerable problems do not simply disappear when they are kept out of sight, and problems that seemed to be solved may continue to rankle – because they were a screen for different problems and the solution was therefore ineffective.

Marital therapists have found that when a couple come to them claiming to have a happy marriage, except for some unhappiness or some dysfunction, some symptom, in one partner, then if the symptom or symptoms are treated, and if the treatment leads to improvement, then the marriage is likely to suffer – because the symptom or symptoms had been helping to stabilise the marriage.

This is done in a wide variety of ways. Sometimes an entire personality is formed to balance or to protect the partner. Sometimes there is an isolated symptom, of greater or lesser severity. An example of the first type would be one person who could maintain his or her dignity only by making the other into a cipher – as in the case of an authoritative husband and meek wife, or a derisive, domineering wife and her hen-pecked husband. The partner who becomes diminished by his or her role may accept it because playing to that role may seem the only way of receiving love, or of being needed, or because he or she is trying to protect the partner from the realisation of his or her own neediness. An example of cooperation in a more specific symptom is that of a woman whose problem seems to be frigidity – but she may be exhibiting this symptom to protect her husband from his anxiety about his own potency. By being frigid, she allows him to feel desire, without challenging him to satisfy either himself or her. He never has to face his own problem. He thinks only about hers.

Typically, the spouse actually encourages the partner's symptoms even while appearing to oppose them, or to seek help in treating them. One man whose wife was afraid to leave the house believed he wanted to cure her phobia, and did indeed consult a professional analyst in an attempt to cure her. But he none the less catered to her phobia by doing all the shopping, running her errands, posting her letters and making it possible for her to accommodate her fear. In treating her symptoms it became clear, however, that she knew her husband was potentially highly jealous, and afraid of romantic competition with other men, and that by staying at home, by assuring him she would never go out, she protected him from anxiety about what she might do, or what might happen to her if she did go out.[2] In another instance, a woman exhibited fear of heights, but it emerged in analysis that her husband suffered severe claustrophobia, a fact which he was able to avoid facing because his wife's fear made it impossible for him to go into lifts with her.[3] Because couples do make these strange arrangements with one another, marital therapists try to treat the couple, rather than one partner, and the person with the symptoms is called the 'identified patient', that is, the member of the family considered by the family as ill. The real patient is the couple, with their invisible loyalties to one another, their fears for one another, their tendency to cover up for one another – and this patient is called the marital dyad.

Who Is the One With a Parents/In-Law Problem?

Couples work together so intimately in the formation of symptoms because projection plays such a prominent part in marriage. This mechanism first developed in infancy, when the child denied his or her own anger and frustration, by seeing it as part of someone else, usually the mother, rather than as belonging to himself. Projection is part of all normal relationships, both for good and ill. We enjoy in our friends those qualities which we would like to admire in ourselves, and we have enemies who represent qualities and characteristics and emotions which we know we have and wish we did not. But projection is not just an attempt to get rid of unwanted feelings. In a complicated way we may need to feel that certain qualities or emotions in ourselves are still part of us even though we cannot quite admit to them. If they are projected onto a family member then they are no longer seen to be ours, but they are not quite lost either. They remain 'in the family', even if we do not admit they are ours. In this way the unwanted feelings and features may become more acceptable to us because they belong to a loved one. They perhaps no longer make us feel guilty, and we can see that another admirable person shares them, and we can eventually tolerate them in ourselves.

Projection is especially powerful in all those relationships that embody the strongest emotional ties – in relationships with parents, children and spouses. It plays an important part in our choice of partner. The theory that we choose a partner who has had a similar family history is incomplete if we do not consider how we choose people who allow us, or encourage us in some way, to see their family history as similar to ours, or to see their psychological development – and arrest – as similar to ours. We need a partner who is able and willing to accept and act out, at least in part, some of what we need to project. This receptiveness can help us, but it can also lead to disaster, as when one partner projects onto the other aspects of the self which frighten him, such as depression or aggression. He needs the partner to express these things for him, but he also needs to denigrate them, and therefore denigrates his partner who becomes a scapegoat for these forbidden feelings. Thus he both hates the partner and is bound to her – because she represents part of himself. The term 'projective identification' indicates this type of attachment within rejection. The repudiation of 'bad' aspects of the self by projection leads one to identify oneself with the person on whom one's qualities or emotions are projected. This may explain why violent marriages are often long-lasting. The partners need one another to have a sense of being whole, even though they also need to attack the other or to be attacked by the other. Each partner values his or her sense of belonging, and the importance he or she plays in the psychological life of the other, so much that they do not wish to escape from the marriage, even though they see how bad it is.

When we understand how projection works in marriage we can see some in-law problems in a totally different light. Spouses can feel so close to one another, can so easily adopt the other's problems and needs and feelings as one's own, that it is often difficult to distinguish problems with parents-in-law from problems with parents. The child-in-law may be the one who is fighting the parents-in-law, but the child-in-law may be adopting the spouse's battle with his or her own parents – a battle which for some reason the partner cannot wage him/herself, either because he/she cannot admit to hostility towards the parents, or because the fear of parental retaliation is too great. There are two cases well known to marital therapists which exhibit this beautifully.

One man consulted a marital therapist because his wife was so aggressive to his mother. He was a quiet, passive man who hated unpleasantness. Also, he saw no just cause for his wife's hostility. His mother, he believed, was self-confident, and used to running a home, but she was not overbearing or excessively intrusive, he claimed. It was true that his mother was demanding, but that was because she was now ill, and his wife was wrong to be so highly critical of her.

At first this seems like a straightforward clash between parental loyalty and marital demands. The husband was protective of his mother and wanted his wife to respect her, yet his wife looked upon the mother-in-law as an intruder who had no right to make demands. The conflict was due to the wife's refusal to offer filial devotion to the mother-in-law, on the one hand, and on the other, the husband's distress at putting his mother in the hands of someone who continually harped upon her own rights, like someone marking out her territory – wasn't it? The husband's distress was a result of this clash of interests – wasn't it?

No, it was not. During therapeutic contact it became clear that the husband's own resentment and anger towards his mother was so incompatible with his love and concern for her that he could not tolerate them in himself. When his mother fell ill, his need to protect her – and himself – from his hostility was doubled. He became more and more ashamed of that hostility and more frightened that it would harm her. Secretly he welcomed his wife's open hostility, because it offered him the opportunity to express, or to have expressed on his behalf, the resentment he himself felt. His wife's outspoken criticisms of his mother gave him the assurance that his own complaints were justified, yet because they were coming from her, he could protest his innocence, and reassure himself that he was loyal and loving. The wife was doing a job for him. He had chosen her in part because he knew she would be good at such a job. However, things got out of hand when he found that even at one remove he could not tolerate 'disloyalty' to his mother. He contacted the therapist on his wife's behalf – the problem was hers, he thought – but of course the problem was his. He knew he needed a partner who would confirm his negative feelings towards his mother, yet he needed such a partner because he could not admit to such feelings, and therefore had to condemn them in his partner, too. The 'mother-in-law problem' could be solved only by coming to grips with his relationship to his mother.[4]

We often are well aware that we are enlisting our partner's help in separating ourselves from our parents. We tend to choose a mate who will understand us, as people, in a way 'our parents don't'. Time and again this emerges as a parent-in-law problem. We want someone to confirm our adult separation from our parents, yet we become distressed when someone does this. But there is another twist to in-law problems, and that is that they can be used in marriage to keep us from feeling too close to our spouse. The blurring of self-boundaries can be disturbing in any relationship, but it is difficult to give the problem a name, or to know how to confront it. Even if one can say that the extensive intimacy between oneself and one's spouse is uncomfortable, what does one do about it? Usually one starts a fight, and it is helpful to know what to fight about in such cases.

One couple saw the mother-in-law as standing between them, and interfering in their marriage. The husband's mother was indeed highly intrusive and domineering. The husband's brother had moved from England to Australia because, it was thought, he could only keep her out of his life if he was at a great distance from her. The couple continually argued about the husband's mother. Theirs was, apparently, the typical mother-in-law quarrel. The husband allowed his mother too much say in their family matters, and the wife allowed her too little. The therapist[5] noted that whenever the couple began to discuss anything about themselves, they began to argue about the husband's mother. The mother-in-law was indeed coming between them, but not in the way they suspected. They were using her to set themselves at a distance from one another.

Many people fear intimacy, because they fear being engulfed by another person. Intimacy may recall, or reactivate, the first relationship with the mother in which self-boundaries had not yet been established. This first relationship may be the prototype of all intimate relationships, and if the task of separation has not successfully been completed, then the infant self – a self without an edge – will creep up on one in any intimate relationship. This blurring of self-boundaries is a good part of intimacy, but if one is unsure about the stability of the self, it may be a threat. Or intimacy may be feared because it makes us especially vulnerable. If we trust a relationship, as we must if we accept intimacy, then we will suffer confusion and pain if the relationship fails. People who have experienced a traumatic loss, or a series of 'exit-type' events in childhood – such as the death of a parent, or abandonment by a parent, or lack of responsiveness due to illness, depression or drug addiction – may have great trouble as adults in achieving intimacy. They want to protect themselves from the pain, from the loss of self that would accompany separation.

The couple who always argued about their mother/ mother-in-law when they began to discuss their problems with one another, were using the mother-in-law to maintain a distance from one another. The husband feared intimacy because, having had an intrusive and domineering mother, he had never been able to feel fully separate from her. Therefore he feared that if he permitted himself to become very close to his wife, then she would engulf him, as his mother had. The wife, on the other hand, feared intimacy for other reasons. She feared the pain of abandonment, and the self-disorientation which follows an important personal loss. Their similar fears, of course, made them compatible, and probably had brought them together. But because they were so compatible, and because they were husband and wife, they found themselves getting too close, and then would separate with a quarrel about the husband's mother. The husband was arguing about his mother in order to keep his wife at a distance, which he had to do because his mother was too close to him. But, as in other cases, his apparent affront at his wife's hostility towards his mother was misguided. She was not exactly expressing his hostility for him, but she was doing a job for him, and she was doing it well. All other family members had had to move far away from the mother in order to be free of her. The husband alone had been able to remain in his native city while having a run at leading his own life. His wife had her work cut out to keep this domineering woman at a safe distance, but she had succeeded. The hostility towards her mother-in-law served the purpose of keeping the mother at a safe distance from her son and of maintaining a safe distance between the husband and wife.

But we can also get on well with our parents-in-law because we want to do our spouse's job for them. Sandra's husband Tim neglected his mother, who in fact agreed that he should devote himself entirely to his career, and should not bother with her. Sandra, on the other hand, visited Tim's mother frequently, and constantly ran errands for her. Was she especially fond of her? Did she feel sorry for her? Apparently not. What she felt was the guilt she believed her husband should feel; and therefore, though she found her mother-in-law snobbish and shallow, she showed a daughter's devotion to her.

She thereby protected her husband's character, and made him guiltless. In this way she also protected herself from facing doubts about her husband's family responsibilities, or indeed about his capacity for love. Good relations with an in-law may be just as complicated, and just as problematic, as bad relations.

We need our spouses to help preserve our adult autonomy. If they fail to do this, they fail us and often the marriage itself fails. There is some case for saying that we need in-law problems because these are so useful in regulating distance from our parents. Ideal relations with one's parents-in-law more often than not signal a weakness in the marriage.

Peter had been attracted by his wife's family as much as by her. His own family was conservative, rigid and avoided demonstrative feelings. His father valued discipline in the home, and believed that a good home was a strict one. His mother was highly strung, nervous and unsure of herself. She would have liked – or so her son believed – to show affection, but was too intimidated by her husband to behave in a manner which might be viewed as 'undisciplined'. Peter, too, was afraid to show affection, and therefore felt guilty towards his mother; but had he shown affection he would have felt guilty towards his father – perhaps because he would have been 'undisciplined' in doing so, or perhaps because he would thereby be setting himself up as a rival to his father. So he remained controlled and cool, but knew that he was being untrue to himself and unfair to his mother. When he met Jacky she was highly and openly attached to her family, who were warm, outgoing and quick to confirm their feelings for one another. To Peter this was delightful, and offered, he hoped, an opportunity to learn how to express affection himself and how to be comfortable with his emotions. It seemed a reasonable hope from what appeared to be a good, complementary marriage.

But Peter's idealisation of Jacky's family, who might release him from his conflicting feelings towards his own parents, was not beneficial to Jacky. At the time of their marriage she had been very attached to her family, but subsequently, she wanted to be more free of them. Because she could get no help with this from her husband, she began to feel trapped within the marriage – because the rule of the marriage was that she remain attached to her family. Nothing negative about her family could be admitted by Peter, and he became distressed and hostile towards her when she tried to separate herself from them. Initially the couple could be described as 'colluding' in their idealisation of the wife's family.[6] Collusion is the process of forming identical inner worlds. One strives to find in the other the embodiment of one's fantasised needs, and the other's cooperation is necessary to sustain this imagined projected identity or image. Peter felt betrayed when his wife tried to break away from the idealisation to greater autonomy, because his wife was refusing to continue to participate in the collusion which Peter needed to give him hope for his emotional development. These complementary partners, from apparently complementary types of families, were eventually at hopeless odds.

In another case where a man's choice of partner was greatly influenced by his attraction to the woman's family, it was the husband who eventually tried to free himself from her family, and as he did so he found that his wife was so tied to her parents that she was incapable of establishing an independent relationship with him. Her father – for whom she worked as an accountant – was a prominent physician, and her husband, as a young physician, was grateful for the help his father-in-law could and did give him. As soon as he set up practice, the young man had the father-in-law's reputation and referrals behind him. This gave him what he called 'an easy ride' and made him feel that his professional success was not his own. When he tried to prove himself on his own footing – he considered moving to another city and starting again – he found no support from his wife. The deeper he looked into the matter, the more profoundly he felt trapped by his and his wife's dependence. There seemed to be nothing between him and his wife but his admiration for her family and his father-in-law's approval of him. His wife had no sense of a life apart from her family of birth. She needed the idealisation of her family that her husband had initially confirmed, and she could make no sense of his need to separate from them, or of his desire that she become more independent of them.

'My Mother Was Right About You . . .'

Sometimes, then, hostility towards in-laws plays a healthy role in the marriage. Sometimes attachment to one's in-laws leads to a stifling marriage. But bad in-law relationships hardly ensure a good marriage. In fact, people with good – or good enough – marriages are usually pretty adept at not going too far. Time and again people told me how they held back in criticising their spouse's family, knowing that once something was said there would be no going back. Or, if a person did appear to make outrageous remarks about a parent-in-law, he or she was usually backed up by the partner, who was in accord with the criticism ('If you knew my mother you wouldn't ask why he has a mother-in-law problem', I was often told). There seemed to be a bar, even in these instances, however, against actually shouting at the parent-in-law: the spouse was encouraged to keep calm, or even to shout at his or her partner, rather than lose his or her temper at a parent-in-law – presumably because this would cause a rift which would be tedious or difficult to mend.

But of course people do go overboard in criticising their in-laws. When this happens, the aim is usually to hurt the spouse, and the quarrel is with the spouse rather than with the spouse's family. Swapping insults about the partner's family may be just another variation of a continuing 'I'm better than you are' battle.

When things go badly in a marriage, each partner mobilises such relatives as are within reach. They need allies against one another. Then the complaint that the mother-in-law is always interfering, or that the partner is always running home to mother, may be that the partner has too much help on her/his side. 'Your mother never liked me', on the other hand, may be spoken in self-pity. It is a way of blaming the spouse's hostility on someone else, rather than on oneself, or on the partnership. And sometimes a person's own despair in the marriage is couched in the language of the parents. 'I should have listened to my mother', or, 'My father was right – you're not the man for me', or 'My parents knew best, after all', are remarks which do not signal the parents-in-law's victory over the spoils of a marriage as much as the child's bewildered recognition of his or her own mistake. In those continuing, destructive marriages we all have witnessed, the in-laws are often alienated because the partners want the field of battle clear for themselves. Relatives might bring some reason to bear, when the partners actually crave their arguments. They cannot tolerate having anyone point out what is going on, how they participate in mutual destruction, how they enjoy their hatred. Or, if one partner feels that he or she lacks the support of parents, then in retaliation the in-laws will have to be alienated – 'it would not be fair', the reasoning goes, 'for him/her to have the support of his/her parents if I haven't the support of mine.'

In bad marriages and in good marriages in-law problems have a role to play in the marriage itself. But this is not the entire story, for there is also the problem the parents have in loving adult children, acknowledging their independence, and seeing them form a new family. I shall look at this problem in the next chapter.

5
How the Innocent Become Outlaws: The Transition from Parent to In-Law

Today, in child development, the emphasis is on the early stages of development, the importance of parenting during the time the child is learning about his or her attachment to other people, and learning whether others' attachment to him or her can be trusted. We hear of the importance of the intense mothering that should occur, to supply the child with self-confidence, psychological stability and the capacity, later in life, to form attachments to others. Because the child does need special care, the parents are primed to give it. Few parents need to be taught how to love their children. They learned from the love their parents gave them. Parents get hooked on their children. The child's well-being becomes linked with their own. But not only do the parents need to see that the child is well cared for, they also need to participate in that care. They need to feel not only that the child is receiving sufficient love but that their child is getting the love from them.

But the child needs something else, too, something which is rarely emphasised by the new wave of child experts who study the phases of attachment and the need for a responsive care-taker. The child needs to separate from his or her parents. The child does this naturally, as he/she experiments with new motor skills and discovers his/her own capacities and prefer-ences and needs. The parents can delight in these new devel-opments and allow the child to feel good about them, and encourage him/her to develop them further, and the parent can also indicate doubt, fear or even despair at separation. Even when the initial hurdle of separation is overcome, when the child knows that he/she is a separate person from the primary parent, there is the further separation which occurs during adolescence – the emergence not only of a separate person but of a person who functions without the domestic support of the family. And this is a very difficult task, as difficult for the child as for the parents.

Adolescence is the crucial period during which, it is hoped, both parents and children acknowledge separation. The ado-lescent, with recent memories of childhood dependence, and still feeling the pull of his parents, is counter-dependent. He or she does everything possible to test or to prove or to assert independence. Usually this comes across as crude self-assertion, or assertion of a self the adolescent is trying to believe in. Friends are sought out because they represent principles, beliefs, assumptions, attitudes which are different from his/her parents. The adolescent's relentless criticism of his/her parents is a way of separating from them or a way of defining a self in opposition to the parents. However patient and understanding parents are, they are at fault, simply because they are the parents, and the child is accustomed to depend on them, and still does depend upon them, but wishes he/she did not. Their approval and disapproval have hitherto represented a power, and the adolescent now resents this, and tries to deny this power, and often, too, tries to demean the value of the parents' love and protection.

At this stormy period of separation, a marriage partner may be sought simply because he or she represents to the adolescent a way of breaking free of the parents, or of asserting that one has different values from the parents, or has a new and different person to rely on. It is easy to imagine the parents' despair at such a marriage, and the in-law troubles that follow. In such cases the parents-in-law are seldom quiet and tactful, but fight tooth and nail to save their child from what they see as a disastrous choice. But the child will fight back with the argument that is unanswerable – the parents are viewing the child's well-being in terms of their values, and in terms of their assessment of his needs, whereas he or she is making a choice on the basis of his or her assessment of his/her needs, and that is the only fair way of making such a choice. At whatever time, at whatever level of maturity one's child chooses a partner, this conflict may arise, and it will usually be argued in this way. The parents cannot justifiably deny that they continue to assess the needs of someone whose needs it had been their obligation and desire to assess for so long. Yet though they may indeed be right, and their child utterly wrong, it is only the child who has the right to make the decision, and only the child's decision will make sense of the marriage.

The Sexual Child

The child's awakened sexuality causes turbulence and confusion not only in him/her but also in the parents. There is the more or less rational fear as to how the adolescent will exercise these strong feelings and desires, but there are also many fears which are less readily admitted and which are disguised as more rational fears. The parent may find himself or herself responsive to the new adult within the child. A father may distance himself from his daughter to protect both of them from his attraction to her. He may be extremely hostile towards her boyfriends because he suspects they want to do what he (perhaps only in part, but because it seems so awful to him, he is unsure that the desire can be contained) wants to

65

do, or because they have access to a relationship with his daughter from which he is prohibited. The mother, typically, tries to remain close to her son, if she is attracted to him, and jealous of his attachment. In such cases any partner will be disliked. Any sexual mate will arouse suspicion and hostility because a mate will be seen as taking something away from the parent.

Any parent who is attached to his or her child – and this is certainly the rule – will feel something of this. It is the parental phase of the Oedipal complex, where they learn that their child can form an intense relationship with someone outside the family, a relationship from which they are excluded. The twist is that the child needs the parents' appreciation of his or her developing sexuality. This gives him or her self-confidence and self-assurance. Yet a parent who becomes jealous as well as admiring makes a bad parent and an impossible in-law.

Sometimes the parents' problems with their adolescent arise from resentment at restrictions they themselves suffered as adolescents, or from the ways in which their own parents curtailed their sexuality, or from the disappointment in their own marriage. Or they are jealous of their previous image as parents – of someone who is strong and protective. Their child's puberty diminishes their importance and power as parents, and they may be reluctant to relinquish them. They may fight with the child in an attempt to preserve their former status.[1]

The battles of adolescence may be far behind when the child does marry. But whenever it takes place, marriage is a declaration that a new family is being formed, another person is now, to the child, the most important family member. Can it be easy for the parents to accept this? They are expected to, because they are adults and probably believe they should be rational. But it cannot be simple.

Parents are accustomed to being physically close to their children. They see their child's mate as someone who is even closer. Are they attracted by the child's mate, or are they repelled by him/her – for whatever reason? Can they cope

66

with the image of their child as anyone's sexual partner? These issues are seldom directly admitted, though they do emerge. 'How can she love him?' one mother asked of me as she paused in her list of complaints about her son-in-law. 'Have you seen him. His hair is all greasy, and his stomach – it hangs like a sack over his belt.' She could not believe her daughter loved him, because she herself found him unattractive. There are many less pronounced examples, too, when the parents are against a child-in-law because he or she does not seem to lie within the range of physical appearance and demeanor which can be seen, by the parents, as belonging to that family. As keen as parents may genuinely be to preserve their values and heritage and beliefs in their children, the strongest and most unanswerable and most unreasonable objection to interracial or cross-religious marriages is that the partner does not look right or act right, that the parents cannot empathise with their child's sexual attraction, and so they cannot empathise with or approve their child's emotions.

Parents' evaluations of their children's attractiveness and sexual appeal also affect their evaluations of their children-in-law. An ideal parent–child relationship involves continuing admiration on every level, but of course ideals are not normal – not because parents fail to love or to value their children, but because they want, and expect, too much from them. They may have wanted their child to be more beautiful, intelligent or accomplished than he/she is. If a parent is disappointed in a child, then the child's spouse will be viewed with suspicion. A highly attractive woman who had one daughter much less attractive than herself was persistently negative about the girl's appearance. 'Don't wear that – you're too fat for it', she would say, without offering any positive suggestion. The daughter's husband was disparaged probably on the grounds that he loved such an 'unattractive' person (though the daughter was less attractive than the mother, she was not actually unattractive), but the real bite in the mother's relationship with the married couple came from the fact that she felt excluded from the love her son-in-law offered her daughter. The mother was naturally ashamed of, and hurt by, her own criticism of her daughter, and she envied the man who was not critical of her daughter, who succeeded in appreciating and admiring where she had failed.

Another woman who considered her daughter to be plain (this emerged in the way she groomed and preened her adult daughter, asking her whether she would put on make-up before she went out, suggesting that she change her dress, which was not thought by the mother to be in fashion, approving of a hairstyle which 'changed her appearance utterly'), idealised her son-in-law. Her unconscious reasoning seemed to be that the son-in-law was good and noble because he had chosen her daughter. In idealising the son-in-law she was trying to placate him. Always, in any argument between the daughter and son-in-law, she took the son-in-law's side, and would privately urge her daughter to compromise in order to avoid a quarrel, and to admit that she was in the wrong, even when she believed herself to be right. The woman had a 'good' relationship with her son-in-law in that it appeared positive and friendly, but the good relationship was based on fear that he would cease to appreciate the daughter, and therefore on the mother's own failure to appreciate her daughter.

Sometimes, however, disappointment in a child can be genuinely alleviated by the choice of a spouse. There may be the hope that the child-in-law will 'help him settle down', or will 'take good care of her'. The parent may understand that his or her disappointment is as much a failure on his/her part as on the child's, and the child-in-law may make the parent willing to relinquish his or her frustrated bid for control, or allay the anxiety of being the only one who will support the child, or stand by him/her through thick and thin.

'I hear your in-laws are coming tomorrow', a colleague commiserated. 'Well, that means no sex for a week.'

Cartoonists depicting mothers-in-law are quick to point out how the mother-in-law's visit interferes with sexual intimacy. A woman's mother breezes in the bedroom with two cups of tea, uttering a brisk 'Good morning,' apparently quite oblivious of the fact that she has intruded upon the couple's love-making.[2] When the parents-in-law visit, they may seem to the child-in-law to be in every bit of the house. 'It's not my home anymore', one daughter-in-law complained. 'My mother-in-law opens the door to my visitors, and my father-in-law takes over the carpenter – whom I've employed.' And the sense of intrusion extends to the bedroom. Tensions between the couple may mount, either because the child is defending his/her parents against the criticism of the spouse, or because the child's own hostility towards the parents is being directed towards the spouse. There may be no sexual contact during the parents-in-law's visit because the couple have no desire. As one woman said, 'When my in-laws come to stay I lose the will to live.'

Sex remains a tricky subject between us and our parents. Sometimes marriage makes sex 'all right', but often marriage is an opportunity to ignore the issue of sex. It is as though the sexual life of a couple cannot be denied if they cohabit, but if they are married, and form a family, then sex can be a sideshow. It may be that the child is reluctant to admit his/her sexuality, that some remnant of the Oedipal phase makes him or her feel as though sex involves a betrayal to a parent. Or it may be that the parents demand such a strong attachment even from an adult child that the child is encouraged to feel guilty about sex, or to feel that sex is a frivolous indulgence. One woman had no trouble expressing her sexual feelings unless she and her husband were staying in her parents' home. Then sexual desire suddenly seemed incongruous to her. She wanted again to be the innocent child, because her father and her relationship with her father – which she felt could be preserved only if she were sexually innocent – took precedence. So it is not only the mother-in-law who may treat the couple's bedroom as a child's bedroom, who interferes with the couple's sex life, but also the entire gambit of parental attitudes and previous needs for the parents' love and approval, or a reactivated and highly outdated sense of loyalty. The parents-in-law's visit may be the loss of one's spouse as an adult, and the visit, too, of a child who has not yet learned to accommodate his/her sexuality or conjugal loyalty. Usually this is partial and temporary. But it is always unpleasant, and it complicates our in-law problems by extending them to marital problems.

Who's Being Selfish?

A parent-in-law's refusal to recognise and respect the child-in-law's sexual relationship with the spouse usually goes along with a refusal to recognise a range of rights, or even an individual identity. It usually stems from excessive possessiveness of the child, because that sexual relationship is final proof of the separation from the parent. Sometimes the parent cannot let go of a child, and so the child's spouse – or any potential spouse – is an enemy. When maternal over-protectiveness is a subject of novels or plays, the emphasis is almost invariably on the relationship between the mother and son or daughter, but sometimes possessiveness emerges only when a spouse or fiancée confronts the parent. There are remarkably few literary works which deal with this subject, but one excellent play, Sidney Howard's *The Silver Cord*, shows all the tactics a mother can use when she faces her daughter-in-law as an enemy and puts up a fight to keep her son. This play is about gracious and ungracious ways of relinquishing people. One scene shows a woman's professor and colleague expressing regret that she is leaving for New York, but also offering his blessing because he knows he has no claim on her. In the next scene she is introduced to her mother-in-law, who ignores her – she is too busy greeting her son and anxiously inquiring after his health. When the son insists that she speak to his wife (he is sure that his mother will love her), the mother-in-law praises her, positively gushes over her, and sits down, pretending to want to talk to her. The mother-in-law feigns enthusiasm for the younger woman's work. She refers to 'archaeology' and then 'geology', pretending to be modest and deferential towards the younger woman's career (she is a microbiologist) but in fact she is dismissing its importance by

70

repeatedly misnaming it. The mother-in-law then shows the couple to their rooms – for various reasons, which make no sense, but which she repeats over and over again as though they did explain something – she puts the husband and wife in separate rooms. Then she describes her plans for her son's career – which of course involve him staying nearby; and when the daughter-in-law protests that her work calls her to New York, where she has received a grant from the Rockefeller Institute, the mother accuses her of being selfish and asking her son to sacrifice his career to hers. The final trump she plays is that which the weak always use against the strong – she is ill, she has a weak heart and if she is left alone she will be destroyed. Like many parents who ask too much from their adult children, she speaks of her many sacrifices and her constant devotion and her decision not to have any interests outside the home because she wanted to give everything to her children.

The parent who speaks of his or her many sacrifices, who becomes a martyr to devotion, is simply trying to bind the child with guilt. Repeated claims that one does not have a selfish bone in one's body and that everything one does is done on another's behalf, are really an insistence that one be paid back for what one has done. Many parents give their children 'everything' so that the children will be endlessly indebted to them, and therefore bound to fulfil their requests. But this is not a valid picture of parental love. Children usually are, in many respects, endlessly indebted to their parents, but to the healthy parent, this is irrelevant. The parent gives his or her child everything because the parent's own interests cannot be separated from those of the child. The parent wants the best for the child as part of what he or she wants for his/her own life. The aim of good parenting should be the independent development of a person, not the production of an adult who must, because of his or her debt, be bound hand and foot to the parent's whims.

There are plenty of real-life instances of this type of mother-in-law trouble. The husband's mother has many complaints about the wife, but complaints would be directed towards any wife, and the point of the complaints and criticisms is to underline the superiority of the mother. An awful competition ensues. Who has more influence? Who has the greater claim? Who has the greater need? The child-in-law may or may not join in the competition, however one-sided, but he/she is always affected by it.

The husband has a terrifically difficult task when his mother does this. Often he tries to be insensitive to it, and often he succeeds, but he tends to make some effort to smooth things over – usually by making excuses to his wife for his mother: 'She is old. She is lonely. She is set in her ways. She can't be expected to change now. What is she really taking from you, anyway? You are the stronger person, and the luckier person – can't you be more generous?' Douglas used all these arguments with his French wife, as she saw herself take second place to her mother-in-law, after her father-in-law's death. Douglas had always been more than normally attached to his mother. He had lived with her until he was over thirty, and had married only when she and her husband happened to take a trip abroad. His mother's spoken criticisms of the young wife were that she was not a good housekeeper, that she was not fertile – and then when she did become pregnant, she remarked that a Scottish woman would not have been so unwell and tired during pregnancy. The mother-in-law herself was frequently ill, with those non-serious complaints of someone oversensitive to her health. She voiced these health complaints in an accusing tone, reminding others of her dependence on them. She dropped many hints about living with her son – if she had family in the house she wouldn't have to worry about this or that casualty – and when she came to visit she would not indicate any date of departure. Finally, with the financial aid of her son, she bought a house nearby. He would visit her on his way home from work, thus arriving home very late. He would say nothing to his wife, but from her point of view it was as though he had a mistress who was acknowledged by them both but never mentioned. In fact, the son was trying to protect his wife from the heavy demands his mother was making on him, and to distance his wife from his mother's constant criticisms. The only way he could remain loyal to them both was to separate them and burden himself by trying to meet each of their claims. Had he shared his burden with his wife she would have felt less excluded and been less hurt, but he would have felt that he was betraying his mother. He had no answer to his mother's claim that she had given birth to him and that he was now the only one she could turn to. His best solution was to sacrifice part of his marriage, or minimise his marriage in a tribute to the guilt she instilled in him.

Sigmund Freud was fond of a parable about an eagle who was carrying her three chicks to safety. She took one at a time over a deep ravine. 'What will you do for me if I fly you safely to the other side?' she asked the chick before starting the journey. The first chick was quiet until mid-flight and then said, 'I will love you and care for you forever.' 'Liar', the eagle remarked and dropped the chick into the ravine. The second chick was asked the same question, and in mid-flight promised, 'I will stay with you forever and do whatever you wish.' 'Liar', the mother remarked, and dropped the second chick. The third chick replied, 'When I am grown and have children of my own, I will look after them and care for them as you are doing for me now.' The eagle did not reply, but carried her last chick safely across the ravine.

Whatever society's expectations for honouring and revering one's parents, the good parent does not try to sustain the intensity of the childhood bond or to exclude other attachments in the adult child's life. In so far as a parent does this, he or she makes a bad parent and a bad in-law. The parent is a bad in-law for the same reason he/she is a bad parent. In trying to make him/herself the primary person in the child's life, the child-in-law becomes the enemy, and the child-in-law has just cause to fear the parent-in-law who will use all former love and all sense of duty to keep the child to him/herself.

This is the cruellest and crudest form of in-law problem. Moreover, most children-in-law who have any kind of problem with their parents-in-law suspect that something like this is going on. They feel their parents-in-law resent their 'ownership' of the spouse, or believe – as I was repeatedly told – that the problem is one of territory, that the basis for all quarrels and complaints is this pull of loyalties and claims.

A spouse who has trouble with his/her parents-in-law will more often than not put it down to the parent-in-law's reluctance to let go, or to the resentment that someone else now has the first claim on their child. But parents cannot be expected, and should not be expected, to give up all concern for their children once their children become adult and form attachments and loyalties to another person. The parent should aim at raising an independent adult, but not an adult for whom the parent no longer has any regard. Because the parent continues to care, the parent will continue to watch and to judge – at least to some degree. How can they not have opinions about how happy their child is, or how far he/she has realised his/her potential, or his/her hopes, and how much all this relates to the spouse? This continuing concern for the child makes it very difficult to be a parent-in-law, who must respect the spouse's position and the spouse's rights and the spouse's influence.

What is a parent supposed to do when, in his or her judgement, a child-in-law is limiting, frustrating or even harming his/her child? Jenny had been determined to teach her son how to function as a responsible member of a domestic household, and he had just about got used to pitching in with housework when he became engaged to a young woman who refused to let him do anything in the house and convinced him he should be waited upon. The prospective mother-in-law remarked that she could not remember when she had found someone who irritated her as much as her son's fiancée. Diane listened in angry amazement as her son-in-law launched on descriptions of all his previous girlfriends. She saw how the husband was trying to threaten her daughter with his ability to attract women, or with his experience of other, presumably more glamorous, women. 'If I said anything, she'd say I shouldn't interfere. So all I can do is tell her how beautiful I think she is, and try to make her feel good about herself. I know it won't mean much if she thinks her husband doesn't like the look of her so much any more. But it's all I can do.' Another woman suspected her son-in-law of beating – or at least frequently striking – her daughter.

> She always protects him, so I don't really know. She tries to be cheerful about it all, as though she has to keep up a front with me – her mother. But I didn't want them to marry. I asked them to wait. And she said she'd never forgive me. So I said, 'Okay, here's my blessing. Take it if you want it.' But she knows I didn't like him, and she won't admit she was wrong and I was right. If I say anything against him, she'll say 'Oh, you're on that kick again.' So maybe I should pretend to like him. Maybe then she would leave him.

Millie, who had weathered a long difficult patch with a daughter-in-law, told me that her mother had been told by her mother that the best thing a mother-in-law can do, if she wants to get on with a child's spouse, is to put a drop of water on her tongue and hold it there. But the mother-in-law's silence does not prevent hostility, and it does not solve problems. What it seems to do, however, is to allow things to change for the better. Her own story bore this out. She has four sons, two of whom are married. Her aim, she explained, was not to love her sons' wives as the daughter she never had, but to appreciate them in their own right – not because they were married to her children. (She had been put out when her own mother-in-law had said, 'Of course I love you. You are married to my son.' This made her feel as though she had no independent identity, as though whatever emotion came her way was as an appendage to someone else, and that it did not matter who she was.) She found young women fascinating, because they were facing problems in a very different way, and were open to many new things. She respected one daughter-in-law, who was a midwife, an active feminist and a part-time journalist. She admired the way the young woman threw herself into something, would dedicate herself to it and learn as much as she could about it. She was absorbed in her pregnancy, but then, when her children were born, seemed to lose interest in spending time with them. The father – Millie's son – became the primary caretaker, and, like most mothers-in-law, she did not like this. But she remembered her own mother's description of a good mother-in-law, and kept her silence and got on well enough with the daughter-in-law – well enough to enjoy her company, to be able to visit and receive visits, and to avoid being a problem within the marriage. Her second daughter-in-law, however, is deliberately aloof and tries to emphasise the superiority of her own family. This daughter-in-law's attitude seems to be, 'I already have a family. I don't need you.' Both sets of the couple's parents live in the same city, and when they visit, they spend all their time with the wife's parents. When Millie makes arrangements for dinner, for the theatre or whatever, the daughter-in-law invariably cancels with the excuse that she has made plans with her own parents.

It would be easy enough, in ordinary circumstances, for Millie to have said, 'Well, bother her', and simply show no interest in her or offer no invitations until the younger woman showed herself more receptive – or at least some sign of politeness. But Millie understood clearly her own dilemma. She could stand up for her rights – and risk alienating the daughter-in-law even more and thereby having even less contact with her son. She said that her own mother and grandmother had been excellent mothers-in-law, that the men their daughters married had come into their families, and felt themselves to be closer to their wives' families than to their own. Of this she had been proud, but subsequently it became a warning to her: mothers could lose their sons to their wife's mother. So she swallowed her pride – as many parents-in-law do – in order to make it possible for her son to come back to her, should he want to. When her grandson was born, her son realised how little contact he had with his own parents. Whenever he and his family visited his native city, they stayed with his wife's parents, and it was his wife's parents who became bonded to the child. To his own parents the child was a charming stranger. He understood why, and he corrected the mistake. He insisted that they stay, for at least part of their visit, with his family, and that his own mother have the child in her home for a full day, whenever possible. So the mother-in-law's silence and patience held out – and of that she is very proud.

Parents-in-law frequently put enormous energy into establishing a good relationship with a child-in-law because they know that if they fail, they risk losing contact with their own child. Parents-in-law can rise above themselves when they do this, overcoming prejudice and pride. One woman said that she was vehemently against the prospect of her daughter, who was white, marrying a West Indian, but when she saw her protests were ineffective she realised that if she continued to state her prejudice, she would be the loser – she would be alienated from her daughter and her grandchildren. Her compromise with prejudice was not tremendous – she said that she still thought coloured folks were awful, but that Vejay was an exception – but for her it was a big stride.

Usually the child-in-law is seen as an enemy when the parent is excessively attached to the child in what appears to be a loving way, but there are some instances in which the parent becomes an enemy of the marriage from resentment towards the child. The son of Rebecca West, the novelist, describes his mother's intrusion in his marriage as a desire to destroy his happiness.[3] The mother, perhaps because she felt that she did not love the son properly, or sufficiently, and because she either felt guilty and ashamed, or cheated of the experience of a close relationship with her son, could not tolerate anyone else being satisfied by and intimate with him. This sounds like a bizarre, grotesque story, but in-law problems as a result of jealousy are really quite common – though they are usually better disguised. A woman who looks around her daughter-in-law's and says, 'I never had all that kitchen gadgetry', and tells her how lucky she is and how much it must help her, may well be expressing hostility and resentment. Also, the martyred mother-in-law, who reminds the child and spouse how much she has done for them, or tells them how much she is doing for them, may be expressing hostility. Her service becomes a way of saying, 'See how much you take from me. Nothing is ever enough.'

In these battles of possession and jealousy it is the mother of the husband or wife, rather than the father, who more frequently is the warrior, because it is she who knows how to use the domestic arena as her battlefield, it is she who is used to reigning in the home, and it is she who is most affected by the attachments of her child, since she for so long was probably his or her primary emotional object. Sometimes the father wages a similar battle, finding all suitors to his daughter unworthy of her, or thinking that their sexual desire of her is in some way wicked, or that their love for her cannot be genuine – because he himself is uncomfortable with his sexual feelings towards her or because he wants to remain the most important man in her life. But usually the bond between father and child does not contain the same potential for blackmail and guilt, and usually – though not invariably – the father is better at letting go.

The Helping Hand

The line between helping a couple and intruding upon them or upon their marriage is very fine. Parents-in-law may be confident they are securely on the helping side, and are aghast to find that their child-in-law has placed them without apology or compunction on the intrusive side. Many people who 'help out' find this. A friend who tries to help out during a marital quarrel will find that neither party welcomes his or her help, and long after the couple have made up their quarrel with one another, the resentment towards the friend's interference will still be felt. But normally a friend, or a brother or sister, can help out in the house without being accused of trying to take power or of being critical or of intruding. Why do parents-in-law have particular difficulty doing this?

I will begin with a simple and apparently innocuous story in which the parents/parents-in-law were trying to help and the daughter-in-law was highly offended by an intrusion.

During the husband's parents' visit to the couple's home they were given a housekey so that they could come and go without checking whether anyone would be in when they returned. At the end of their visit they left without returning the key. This type of oversight is common enough, and it would be unfair to insist that there was a motive behind it. But some time later, when the couple were away on holiday, the husband's parents used the housekey to 'check up on the house', and in doing so, they worked in the couple's garden, planting spring bulbs as a nice surprise.

The daughter-in-law was outraged. Well that just shows how unreasonable she was, doesn't it? The husband's parents, after all, were trying to help out. They were trying to be nice. They were being nice, planting those bulbs. There's just no appreciation from a child-in-law.

But the daughter-in-law was justified. This was her home, and her parents-in-law's 'help' denied this. Their unsolicited help, their use of a housekey that had not been given them, but merely loaned to them for their convenience during a visit, showed that the parents-in-law had little sense of the younger woman's proprietary rights. Their gesture was intrusive and controlling – all the more so because they could not see the insult in their actions. The daughter-in-law was outraged not because she thought that her husband's parents had intended any harm, but because they had neglected to respect her privacy.

Being helpful and being intrusive – the line marking the difference is particularly fine for in-laws to draw. This is not to deny that parents-in-law can be enormously helpful, but their help is often problematic. One reason may be that between the parents and the child there are cross-generational boundaries which tend to be respected. These boundaries generate rules whereby the child, for example, would not, as an adult, intrude upon his or her parents' gardening plans, since he/she acknowledges the parents' views, but the parents might offer suggestions and assistance in the child's garden. As a child one almost certainly grew up with the notion of a generational pecking order, whereby the parents' views and decisions were most important, and their privacy was respected. Parents must learn to offer their grown-up children something of the same respect, but lapses, or areas of interference, are permitted and even desired, as an indication that the parents retain some of the former intimacy and concern. But the child-in-law does not usually share this indulgence. As an adult, as half of a married couple, he or she is intent upon establishing his/her own home, with rules that suit him/her, and with a good portion of control. The deference that the spouse owes to his/her parents is not easily, and certainly not automatically, transferred to the parents-in-law. Usually, when people become parents-in-law, they understand this. My own mother-in-law can be absurdly deferential when she visits me in my home, asking permission to use my bathroom, or inquiring whether I mind the suitcase remaining in the hall for a few minutes – but then, an hour later, she will invite a friend to my house without asking my permission, or will organise a dinner party in my home and treat me like a guest at my own table. Even when a parent-in-law tries to show his or her child's spouse proper deference (and not all parents-in-law try to do this) there remains the assumption that he/she has certain parental rights over the child-in-law's home – and sometimes over his or her life-style.

People frequently insist that 'being nice' or 'being helpful' is the most important description of their behaviour, when they are really working very hard to get their own way, and the wishes of the recipients of these 'nice' actions are at best secondary. Being nice can lay down the terms of a placatory bargain: 'If I am nice, and if I compliment you, telling you that you are nice, too, then I have set a standard which I expect you to keep; you must be nice because I am, and because I have told you that you are, too.' Being nice and helping out can also be ways of getting attention: 'See how much I'm doing for you', and perhaps the expectation is, 'Now it is your job to thank me.' The other side of this behaviour might be the hostile attitude, 'See how much I've put myself out for you' or 'See how much⸳ you owe me.' Parents-in-law, like all people, often want to help out because they want to be included in someone's life (a kinder and equally valid description is that they want to share in others' lives) but then are put out when the couple – in particular the son- or daughter-in-law – sees their behaviour in terms of what it is doing for the parent-in-law, as opposed to what it was meant to do for them. The outraged daughter-in-law saw that her husband's parents wanted a share in her home. The parents-in-law were therefore intrusive. Her parents-in-law saw themselves as helping in the home. The daughter-in-law was therefore ungrateful. The two parties could not understand the other's frame of reference.

It is hard to have one's best intentions scrutinised so cruelly. After all, even when parents-in-law intrude, they may not intrude with any malice. What harm have we done even if we did 'invade their privacy' they may ask, whereas the person whose privacy has been intruded upon may think that the question is irrelevant, and the principle is the most important issue.

There is another complication, which may persuade us that a helpful in-law is committing some crime, and that is the difficulty we have in general with accepting help. An old Jewish joke underlines this. Nathan tells Joel that David is angry with him and no longer wants to have anything to do with him. Joel asks in amazement, 'What did I ever do for David that he should be so angry with me?'

From parents we are used to accepting gigantic favours. We know parents are acting for themselves when they act on our behalf, because our well-being is linked to theirs. Also, in our culture, gratitude is not required. We are allowed to take parents for granted, and we are allowed to take as much as they will give. But help from a parent-in-law, though offered with a parent's goodwill, is not as free from strings as a parent's help: the greater the help offered, the greater the problems which arise between the in-law who receives and the in-law who gives.

A notable case of a parent-in-law's help backfiring is that of

81

Philip Graham, former editor of the *Washington Post*, and his father-in-law, Eugene Meyer, former owner of the *Post*.[4] Eugene Meyer was an aristocratic German Jew, whose patriarchal attitudes did not permit him to pass on the newspaper to a woman, even if that woman was his daughter. The best thing this highly intelligent and socially awkward daughter did for her father was to marry the charming Philip Graham. Like most people who knew him, Eugene Meyer was enthralled by Graham. He saw the son-in-law as his true son and, like a domineering father, he wanted Graham to have all he could give. He hoped that by giving all, Graham would fulfil his own dreams. He persuaded Graham to accept editorship of the *Post*, a job which initially held for Graham the appeal of a challenge. Subsequently, the fact that he had been given it and not earned it, tainted everything. Though Graham became a highly successful and innovative editor, his achievements never seemed to belong to him, because of his initial debt to Meyer. The *Post* owner had given Graham, rather than his daughter, the majority of the voting stock precisely to avoid any sense of dependence, but the excessive generosity defeated its purpose. We wage many battles with our own parents for independence, and they too can interfere with our adult autonomy by helping us too much and continuing to give us too much, as though we were still children, but the gifts of a parent-in-law bring with them unexpected bitterness. Once, when a friend of Graham's refused to accept a loan, Graham chided him, 'Listen, don't kid yourself. We're all beholden. Have you ever looked at my life?' He never escaped the burden of his father-in-law's generosity. It interfered with his marriage – Kate Graham was to be insulted repeatedly by him, because she had, through her father, given him too much, and been denied too much, by her father, on his behalf. Towards the end of his life Graham ranted against Eugene Meyer, too, complaining that his father-in-law had never truly appreciated him, and had never given him credit for what he had done. But it was Graham who could not give himself credit for what he had achieved because his autonomy had suffered the fatal wound of his father-in-law's help.

Few cases of receiving help are this troublesome, but few, too, are without complications. How much we can tolerate being helped by our in-laws depends upon how secure we are in our adult identity, and how we tend to view our achievements – must they be ours alone, or can we accept that someone has contributed to them? It tends to be fathers and sons-in-law who face this problem, since it is usually fathers-in-law who help sons-in-law in a professional capacity. But the problems surrounding help and intrusion are more frequent between daughters and mothers-in-law because parents-in-law tend to concentrate their help within the domestic setting, where, typically, the woman is more possessive. The touchiness inherent in the situation – two women who have known the man (husband/child) intimately, may well explode at apparently trivial issues. 'You really should rinse Peter's shirts several times', a woman told her daughter-in-law as they were hanging out the washing. 'He has very sensitive skin.' Most daughters-in-law would rankle at this, and most daughters-in-law face a barrage of similar helpful suggestions during a visit from their parents-in-law. 'Wouldn't John prefer tea in the garden?' 'You have plenty of room in this house. That big upstairs room needn't always be your study. There's no need to move just yet, is there? Not that I would dream of interfering. I just think you already have a nice house.' I once heard my mother-in-law tell her daughter to suggest that her husband build a cupboard in the guest bedroom, but advised her to wait for a while, because if she made the proposal immediately after their visit he would suspect that his in-laws had been intruding. She could understand that someone would suppose her to be intrusive, but she could not admit that she was actually being intrusive.

Heart-to-Heart

Since these and many other in-law disputes involve different interpretations of behaviour, rather than direct clashes of interest, wouldn't open discussion help clear the air? Often insults are felt, when no insult was intended. Would not the wound be healed by careful explanation? And when it came to more general issues, too, wouldn't it be best if people just sat down and talked? What if the woman, Millie, with four sons, explained to her aloof daughter-in-law that she respected her attachment to her own family, but that this attachment should allow the daughter-in-law to understand how hurt the mother-in-law was at the prospect of losing her son to his wife's family. She could explain her willingness to share, and try to persuade her daughter-in-law that this could be done, that the families need not be in competition. Bringing this out in the open would, at the very least, make it more difficult for the daughter-in-law to get away with her rudeness. At best, it would give her a fuller understanding and respect for her mother-in-law's feelings.

Alas, frankness as a problem-solver is greatly overrated. In my experience, an open discussion of in-law complaints was not effective. 'My mother-in-law said "Can we have a talk?" and the hairs on my arm stood on end. I could feel the electricity in the room, and I knew she was ready for a downpour', Alice, Millie's daughter-in-law, told me.

She wanted to hold a hearing of her grievances. She led me into the den and shut the door, and I couldn't concentrate on what she was saying. I felt she had the upper hand, because she had initiated the talk, and because it was in her house, and because she knew what she was going to say. I had to find a way to protect myself! So I kept repeating, 'Of course. All right', just to end it all. And I really hated her for a while after that, because she had humiliated me.

Not all people involved in in-law tensions are as articulate as Millie and her daughter-in-law, but many of them clearly respond similarly. When Meg telephoned her mother-in-law, after discovering she had used the borrowed housekey to visit the house and plant bulbs in their absence, she wanted to explain her view, and to protect her privacy, or her territory, in the future. It seemed a reasonable thing to do, and was a reasonably positive approach. It meant, after all, that she was not writing her mother-in-law off, that she was giving her a chance to defend herself, and giving her a chance to avoid future bad feeling. But, human nature being what it is, the mother-in-law did not see it this way. 'Well I'm sorry', she declared, in that defensive tone which is actually a denial of an apology. 'We were only trying to help. How could we be intruding if you weren't even there?' Meg's response was denied validity, so, from her point of view, she had a further insult to contend with, while her mother-in-law felt insulted too, and now had grounds to be suspicious that any action would be negatively construed.

Arguments – out-and-out quarrels – between in-laws are very tricky. Who will referee them? What side will the son or daughter take? What right has someone outside the family to criticise one – or, indeed, why should someone within the family criticise one as though one were a stranger? And what happens in an argument when too much is said? Where does the son or daughter stand in relation to his or her parents when they stomp out of the house after a quarrel with the spouse? This fear puts the lid on many arguments, though not on bad feelings or a sense of grievance. Because a straightforward quarrel might prove painful, not only for the arguing parties but for the spouse who must somehow feel involved, in-laws tend to express complaints indirectly or even deviously. Meg's father-in-law, on a subsequent visit, referred to someone as 'that Irish bitch', well aware that Meg was Irish. He could deny he was getting back at her (he was not after all referring to her, and he was not saying that all Irish women are bitches), while none the less putting her on edge. Confrontation between in-laws, it seems, does not lead to a fair showing of one's hand, but to further hostility and deviousness. The difficulty is that the apparent complaint, or the apparent issue, is the tip of the iceberg. Pride, loyalty and a sense of one's proper place within the family are involved. In becoming an in-law, one may suddenly find oneself part of a grotesque competition, wherein strangely inconsequential things become significant and the rules are always being defined by someone else. No wonder it is a relationship in which we frequently exhibit adolescent touchiness and negativism.

6
Claustrophobia: In-Laws versus Self-Identity

We wage awful battles for separation and individuation from our parents. As adolescents our hostility towards them stems from the belief that they are crippling our ego. We feel invaded by them, and at the same time they appear to be inside us, they deny what we believe to be truly there. As adults we have usually achieved some autonomy, and we no longer need to hate our parents. We have greater options for attachment figures, and we choose friends who enforce or perhaps flatter our self-image. Our marriage partner is particularly important in this respect. A good partner will stimulate the best aspects of our independence, and will help us grow. A poor partner will limit us, enforce our weakness and defensiveness, thus inhibiting our growth. But even the best partner brings with him or her images of former threats and new impediments to our development. Every marriage partner is accompanied by parents – by his or her attachment to them, and by the parental authority they represent. Every marriage, therefore, presents new opportunities of growth alongside new attacks against us.

Role Prescription

The family is a system. The members of a family do not behave randomly towards one another. The behaviour of each influences and is influenced by the other's. Actions, feelings, expressions can be seen as part of a network. In some families the emphasis is on homeostasis – on maintaining the system as it is. The members, or the dominant members (usually the parents), fear change. Anything which might bring about change produces a 'negative feedback' – that is, a change in the system which is geared to keep the system as it was. A father who sees his daughter growing away from him, for example, might change the manner of his authority. Whereas he had been confident and calm in his discipline, he may now exhibit a stern and dictatorial manner in order to sustain his authority. He changes his tactics so as not to change something he values more. A mother who fears quarrels above all else may change her attitude towards various prohibitions in order to preserve harmony. A child who fears his mother's and father's quarrels, or fears that they will separate, may become a 'problem' child in order to keep his parents' attention focused on him; hence they stay together, and do not focus on their dissatisfactions with one another. Sometimes families all work together to keep things just as they are. After a stimulating holiday, or a stressful upheaval, they may pride themselves on getting back to a routine by saying, 'It's as though we never went away', or 'It's as though we never had a fire.'

In more open systems, changes may produce 'positive feedback', leading to development and adaptation. In the sparse research that has been done on 'happy' families – in contrast to the mountains of research done on disturbed families – it was found that families without marked problems, families in which the members could function normally, were far more receptive to new ideas, that they were capable of sustaining contradictory viewpoints and feelings without distress, that there was greater respect for difference both within and without the family, and greater autonomy among the members of the family system.[1] Severely dysfunctional families, on the other hand, could tolerate only a narrow range of responses. Little attention was paid to individual perception and feeling, or to any view that did not fit the family's collective thoughts – and often the collective thoughts were decided not by consensus, but by a dominant member. Sometimes the system was kept stable through intimidation, or sometimes one member showed such marked signs of distress at certain changes that the other members denied or covered up the change in order to protect her/him from anxiety.

One member of the family may be accustomed to do most of the work of maintaining the system, but the members of the family usually work together. They have established ways of keeping the system as they think it should be kept – of grooming out kinks, keeping certain doors closed and making sure certain dogs stay asleep. The methods of maintenance are themselves important parts of the system. A dismissive chuckle here, an anxious grunt there, a glare, an encouraging smile may be enough to keep things in order, to indicate what feelings or attitudes are allowed, what expressions arouse fear and what behaviour is to be condemned or endorsed. The son or daughter, having grown up, developed in and perhaps survived such a system will have a pretty clear knowledge of how to take what comes up in the family, how to protect himself or manoeuvre herself. A daughter- or son-in-law, however, comes upon the scene unprimed for these domestic manipulations, which are peculiar to each family. Even if we have chosen a partner who is very like us in terms of which feelings are admissable and which feelings and fears one needs protection from, the methods of enforcing what remains 'behind the screen' will probably be different. And if we have had the gumption to choose someone who jars our perimeters, then our partner's family is bound to shock or irritate us.

Ruth, a lawyer, with two young children, took a deep breath and said, 'What I am going to tell you sounds impossibly petty. I don't know what I'm complaining about. Yet at the end of a three-day visit with my parents-in-law I was a basket case.'

The strong feeling, in conjunction with her belief that it had no basis, was striking in this normally rational and gracious woman. I asked her to reconstruct at least one situation which had infuriated her. She put together a scene which took place at breakfast, the day after Christmas.

The breakfast table had been, as usual, neatly laid by the mother-in-law. Ruth's six-month-old baby had been up since 5 a.m., and Ruth tried to quieten her, hoping to save the rest of the household from disturbance. At half-past seven, the baby dozed off, and Ruth slept for an hour. When she came down to breakfast her husband was already at the table.

Mother-in-law: 'Ah, good morning, Ruth? You've have a good rest. Stephen, we can start. Ruth's come down.'
Ruth: 'You didn't have to wait for me.'
Mother-in-law: 'Oh, but we wanted to. Cereal?'
Ruth: 'Thanks.'

Ruth takes the bowl that is offered and pours milk from the jug. The mother-in-law pours out her own cereal, picks up the jug, and then puts it down without pouring any milk. She then places her bowl at her husband's place.

Son: 'What are you doing, Mum?'
Mother-in-law: 'I'm just worried there isn't enough milk. You used more yesterday than I expected. I suppose Ruth needs to drink a lot. But the milkman will be here soon.'

Stephen, the father-in-law, now comes to the table. It is usual for him to choose his own cereal, and to pour it himself. He looks at the bowl at his place.

Mother-in-law: 'I poured it for myself but we haven't enough milk. Your need is greater than mine.'

She laughs. The father-in-law grunts, opens the jar of cereal and pours the cereal in the bowl back in the jar. He takes a plate for toast.

Ruth: 'Why didn't you tell us you were low on milk? I wouldn't have minded not having cereal. And I don't particularly object to black coffee, either, but you've poured me two very milky cups.'

Mother-in-law: 'I wanted you to have a nice breakfast.'

Ruth: 'But I would have liked to have a choice.'

Father-in-law: 'So you've found something else to criticise her for, have you? Next time you'll know [turning to his wife] not to give her breakfast.'

Are the issues here really petty? I don't think so. They concern questions about who is considered generous, who is allowed to think of others, and who is the one who takes eveything for granted.

The son was the first to spot something strange in his mother's behaviour. If he had not asked what she was doing when she put down the jug and changed the bowl from her place to her husband's, Ruth would not have noticed anything. The son's query is a spontaneous display of irritation. He sees something is out of place. When he understands what it is, he is no longer concerned. But the daughter-in-law's interest is then caught. The son can accept a favour from his mother in a way that she cannot. The mother-in-law's behaviour makes her feel guilty, and she becomes angry because the guilt is gratuitous. The father-in-law nearly falls into the same trap as he is about to take the cereal, but he too sees something is amiss and this gives the mother-in-law a chance to explain herself to her husband and to define her role again as someone who always puts another's needs before her own. Ruth's spirits were no doubt firmly depressed given that she had been up during the small hours of the morning trying to keep her baby quiet on her parents-in-law's behalf. Coming down she meets the mother-in-law, fresh from a good night's sleep, who tells her – not asks – that she has had a good rest, and then comments on how much she has done for her. Then the father-in-law takes a sudden swipe at her by refusing to see her point about wishing she had had a say in who gets the milk and who holds back. By refusing to understand her, he takes his wife's part and supports her caring role, enforcing the image of the daughter-in-law as someone who is always carping. In the end, what is surprising is not how irritated people can become about small matters, but how ingenious they can be in bringing important matters to bear upon petty ones. Clearly, the family work together and Ruth is both an outsider and a member. She is an outsider because she does not immediately see the game and is unable to protect herself from the role in which she is being cast. She is a member in that, unlike a guest, she is not quite entitled to the mother-in-law's sacrifice, which has a different meaning in regard to her than it would in regard to a guest.

The skill with which families define their members' roles is remarkable. How does one member resist the dominant members' prescriptions? It would take some time for Ruth to explain to her parents-in-law what they were doing – and it is unlikely she could do so herself, in the heat of the moment. Even her husband, in all probability, would tire of the effort, and she would be seen by all of them to be making heavy weather of something that was really of no consequence. At this stage in the proceedings – when the in-laws are doing such a good job at putting the outsider in her place – the only response available is carping or sulkiness or counter-criticism which seems unfair because it is not really to the point. Someone in Ruth's position might take a high hand in other matters – for example in her political views – just because she feels opposed to everything or anything her parents-in-law might say. The persistent objections from a son- or daughter-in-law, which people find so confusing, so wearing and so unwarranted, may be the son- or daughter-in-law's attempt to get back at them for being so good – and so unfair – at defining him or her in their terms and for their purposes, and denying the identity he/she believes should be recognised within his or her family.

Disaffirmation and Denial

We may be adults. We may believe ourselves to be secure. Yet there are always points of self-identity about which we are less rather than more sure, and there is nothing like continuous, indirect, velvet-gloved assault to make us aware of these weaker points.

Often the work against us is more tenuous and less conclusive than role dictation. In a family which functions as a system for the purpose of permitting some attitudes and emotions and denying others, our own attitudes and emotions, our hopes and views, may well lie outside the permissible. Someone who is accustomed to open criticism may feel stifled by his/her in-laws' belief that criticism is dangerous. The in-laws will ignore such discussions, or treat them as a joke. Someone who craves a soft approach to problems may be more shattered than any family member when the father-in-law slams his fist on the table or the mother-in-law shrieks at her child. The explosion might have nothing to do with the child-in-law, and yet the child-in-law might be utterly thrown by it.

The different emotional temperature, the different views on politics or religion, the different gauges of good and bad feelings, permissible and forbidden thoughts, are not merely differences of opinion or different customs. They involve different views of what we are and what we should be. The knowledge that the people close to us will not accept our feelings and ideas – in the sense that they will not be heard, or that they will be dismissed before being heard, or that they will be ignored – leads to a sense of disaffirmation. The frustration of this cannot be overestimated. For children it is crippling. If their parents persist in this practice then they will be ashamed of their own feelings, and confused as to how to handle their shame. Children-in-law come into the family as adults and are therefore less vulnerable, but denial behaviour is still supremely irritating. In defence one may decide to pay back one's in-laws with similar denial behaviour – never treating their remarks seriously, constantly finding fault with them, pretending to know better just because one may be better educated. Or perhaps the parents-in-law dole out such punishment to the son- or daughter-in-law because they fear that he or she, with the help of their own child, will in some way, and for some reason, dismiss them, and deny their assessment of themselves.

Self-identity and self-respect are difficult to sustain in any family relationship. The people closest to us want us to be people who will meet their needs. They encourage in us traits they hope we will continue to exhibit. They ignore qualities we ourselves may value but are of no use to them. They construct fantasies about what we are, either because they need us to be good or because they need us to be bad, and they treat us accordingly. When we feel we have no link with the person they take us to be, we may feel not only frustrated and ignored, but annihilated. Often this network of desires and fantasies works for us too, and usually we contribute to it and get something from it. For the most part they love us, and we love them and need to be what they need us to be, and have perhaps chosen them because they are able to see us as we need to be seen. But in regard to in-laws we face one grave disadvantage. We do not come first. Our needs, or even what our in-laws suppose to be our needs, are not their primary interest. They are interested in, and care first for, the needs of their children: the son- or daughter-in-law is an adjunct to these.

If the son- or daughter-in-law is persuaded to consider her- or himself as a natural child, or just like the parents-in-law's own child, then he or she must face an impossible sibling rivalry, where the parents' concern lies with another child. The constructions and avoidances in the parents-in-law's view of the son- or daughter-in-law will be doubly insulting because they are geared to the well-being, or to the hypothesised well-being, of someone else. The individuality which we in our culture prize so highly will be cruelly slighted, and the parents-in-law, while perhaps being generous in their thoughts, eager to see the good of their child's spouse, will none the less be committing the crime of failing to see the spouse's distinct personality. In the presence of the parents-in-law, therefore, the spouse is likely to experience the utmost claustrophobia, as he or she is closeted not merely with another's view of him/her, but with another's fantasies based upon their assessment of another's needs.

It is not surprising, for example, that a parent-in-law would have little sympathy for a son-in-law who, in middle age, made a decision to abandon a secure job, sell the family house and travel with the family in order to get a better sense of direction or a firmer grasp on priorities. Greg's parents-in-law saw this behaviour as self-indulgent and selfish; their daughter, who supported her husband's decision, could not persuade them that he was not harming her. From Francine's point of view, her husband's well-being was as important as her own, and she was glad to participate in his 'male meno-pause', as her parents described it. But from her parents' point of view, she was being asked to take an unwarranted risk, and a needless cut in income. The son-in-law's personal needs did not seem to them more important that their daughter's and grandchildren's material comfort. They had believed themselves to be fond of Greg, but their responses showed how they viewed him as a provider for their daughter, rather than as a person who had a right to seek his own potential. Sometimes the parents-in-law's response may be more extreme. When Joanne felt she needed a 'marriage sabbatical', and decided to take courses as a resident student in a university town 150 miles from her family home, her mother-in-law became convinced that she was clinically insane. She telephoned the local authorities, consulted a psychiatrist and eventually notified the police. Her son, however, was fully able to cope at home. The children were nine and twelve, and could help him with the new domestic arrangements. He was not delighted by his wife's behaviour, but he understood it and was willing to accept it. His mother, however, could not tolerate his limiting his career energy, and perhaps some career opportunity, on account of his wife's need for further development – which she sought through further education and a reprieve from domestic demands. The daughter-in-law's needs simply did not appear that important.

Objections to a son- or daughter-in-law's interests, or undermining his or her identity, may be far more subtle – and, for that very reason, more stifling. Sonia dreaded contact with her mother-in-law, and looked upon her visits as 'dead time', yet the only concrete complaint she had was that her mother-in-law never mentioned her work. Sonia worked in the civil service, at a rank equal to that of her husband, who worked in a different department. The mother was proud of her son, and spoke of his achievements (especially when his work was related to the Falkland's crisis), but spoke to her daughter-in-law only about domestic matters, and indicated that her most important role was that of housekeeper. This attitude emerged in a myriad of apparently insignificant slips. 'I'd like to save you a job', she said, during a visit, 'can I iron some of Chris's shirts for you?' They had a full-time house-keeper whom the mother-in-law simply did not see, nor could she recognise that the domestic set-up was such that it was not the daughter-in-law's job to iron the husband's shirts. She would praise the daughter-in-law for preparing a meal so well, when in fact Sonia had come home five minutes before the family sat down at the table, and her husband had been more involved in the preparation than she. The mother-in-law responded to Sonia as though she were what she thought she should be; she thereby 'nothinged' the real Sonia.

The clash between different generations' expectations of a woman's priorities and woman's identity provides much fuel for mother-in-law/daughter-in-law conflict. Whereas a mother will probably be proud of a professionally successful daughter, even though there may also be some rivalry between them, or some sense that the daughter's success puts the more traditional mother in a poor light, a mother-in-law will tend to be put out by the daughter-in-law's refusal to communicate with her along expected lines (how to run the home, raise children, etc.) or may be at sea as to what to say because she fears that traditional topics are ruled out. For the daughter-in-law, forging a different kind of female identity, the mother-in-law's slips may be particularly irritating because they threaten her with the weight of female stereotypes. Perhaps Sonia's mother-in-law simply did not know how to speak to another (let alone a younger!) woman about her professional life. Yet the effect of her avoidance was to deny the reality of her daughter-in-law's career.

My own mother-in-law has developed a marvellous way of combining recognition with denial of my work. She knows I often take advantage of their visits as time I can use to be free of the children. As she was planning an outing with them she asked, 'Are you coming with us, or would you like a lazy day at home so you can get on with your writing?'

Comedy fails to soften the insult, however, when the attack is on the daughter-in-law's suitability as a mother, or the well-being of the children. 'Your life will soon change', Rachel's mother-in-law laughed as a family dinner was interrupted because she had to leave for an emergency meeting with the US Secretary of State, for whom she was a speechwriter. Rachel was pregnant, and earlier in the evening the mother-in-law had fingered her designer cashmere jacket and remarked, 'You'll soon be spending your money on other things.' But the behaviour which Rachel decided was 'unforgivable' took place several years after the birth of her first child – when her second child was a year old, and she was still working.

I've had the same nanny since my first boy was six weeks old. But however long she works for me, however well I know her, I cannot be sure that she is not really cruel to the children when I'm at work. They seem to like her, and she seems to love them. But what actually goes on when I'm at work? I can't know.

She was shaking so hard as she spoke that she had to set her wine glass on the table.

> My mother-in-law, who had stayed at home all day while I was at work, told me that the nanny had been getting at the children all day – that she threatened to spank them – that she called my older boy a liar. I was so upset that I did something I know was rather gross. I took the nanny and the children aside and cross-questioned them. It's hardly the thing to aid happy relations between us, but my judgement was not particularly sound at that moment, and I did it.

The result of the informal hearing was that the nanny had told the younger child, when he claimed to have finished using the potty, 'No, you're not finished', and Rachel confirmed, 'It's your loss if you believe him when he says that.' The nanny had prevented the older child from pulling down the chair cushions to construct a tent while she was hoovering the carpet. 'A sentiment I might express myself', Rachel added wrily. Yet the mother-in-law's description of the day at home – just the thing Rachel could never witness – continued to rankle her, because it prodded the working mother's deepest and most recalcitrant fear – that children are suffering because she works.

The Good Behaviour Syndrome

'She's too nice', is often a genuine and vehement complaint about a mother-in-law. She is trying too hard, finding everything just too jolly, complimenting one too much, being too helpful and too, too kind. It is not the sweetness that is wearing, however, but the manipulation, denial and fear that make such thick icing necessary.

Not parents-in-law alone, but sons- and daughters-in-law, too, get caught up in a good behaviour syndrome. They are desperate to please, over eager to be pleased – all because they are all too familiar with in-law stereotypes and wish to deny them. The symptoms are easily spotted. The daughter-in-law solicits domestic advice. The son-in-law listens to the father-in-law's assessment of the world, daring to swallow the meat he has been chewing for the past five minutes only after the father-in-law has finished speaking. The mother-in-law compliments the daughter-in-law on her house or on her dress, and the daughter-in-law returns the compliment. The conversation is thick with leading questions and tag questions. 'You must have enjoyed your holiday', or 'You must be pleased with your new house', or 'Isn't this a lovely photograph?' or 'Weren't you lucky to get the decorating done so quickly?' and 'You have a lovely view, haven't you?' As a result, one's responses are severely limited. No one can escape the ultra-positive atmosphere because the conversation does not permit any difference of opinion or any true individuality – because individuality is dangerous and might spark hostility. The conversation keeps everything under control because there is a mutual agreement not to be in touch with one's real feelings. One does not want to face another's feelings, which might somehow be insulting or shocking or embarrassing. One does not want to be too closely in touch with one's own feelings, either, because they too might arouse unpleasantness, and so one is glad of those interlocking exchanges which make the appropriate response not only obvious but essential.

Of course there is the drawback that, for most of us, communicating only about super-safe issues, and being so out of touch with ourselves, are very tiring. Not only do such defences demand a good deal of nervous energy, but one eventually feels insulted (after all that work to avoid insult!) that such defences are required. Why do they have to work so hard to like me? one may wonder. Why can I only say what they prod me to say? Are my own responses so unacceptable? Would we really quarrel so horribly if we strayed onto topics that involve us, or if we let our thoughts and feelings be known? The ultimate effect of the good behaviour syndrome is to make us believe that the answer is, 'Yes, spontaneity would destroy acceptance.'

If one person does try to bring greater individuality into the conversation, other members have ways of keeping control. In my own family, my mother-in-law's skill is paramount. Her son frequently tries to jar her recalcitrantly nice sentiments, but does so in the form of teasing, so that she can treat his remarks as playfulness and dismiss them as such. If my husband swears, or speaks sharply, she laughs and exclaims, 'David!' as though to say, 'What a naughty little boy you're being.' If I say something which jars her, she hesitates for a moment, then decides I am joking, and laughs twice, in descending triplets. Recognition of others is an acceptable sacrifice, when harmony is at stake.

Why is the sacrifice necessary? What lurks behind the harmony? Is it a difference of opinion on the floor covering – or on politics or religion? Sometimes. Sometimes different religions, different political views, different nationalities or races involve such profound feelings that divergent opinions cannot be tolerated within one's family, and if one is to give another person a fair chance as a family member then these topics must be avoided. In such circumstances one denies or avoids certain topics in order to make personal contact. But more often than not the danger point is in the relationship itself, and what is avoided is personal contact. For sons- and daughters-in-law always face the prospect of the cruellest criticism when they face their parents-in-law – they face the assessment that they are 'not good enough'. And parents-in-law may worry about this too, and want to 'make a good impression' and avoid 'disappointing their son/daughter' by failing to impress his/her spouse or fiancé; but more commonly they fear being identified as the disapproving in-law, an image which, after all, may be as hard to identify with as to confront. It has been described perfectly by D. H. Lawrence in *St Mawr* where Mrs Witt, the mother-in-law, 'kept track of everything, watching as it were from outside the fence, like a potent well-dressed demon, full of uncanny energy and a shattering sort of sense'. We see 'her terrible grey eyes with the touch of a leer' looking on, revealing her contempt. How many happy, anxious gleams are pinned to a parent-in-law's eyes in order to avoid this description?

The image of a monstrous, disapproving observer must be denied, because usually it is valid. No one is really good enough for a parent's child. There is a narcissistic commitment to one's child which may be kept in control by reason, or may be well covered by disappointment, or may be denied because it is not in keeping with a parent's view of him/ herself, but it is none-the-less present. Along the spectrum of the good behaviour syndrome – which ranges from giving someone an extra good chance, because he/she is married to someone one loves or is closely related to one's partner, to being totally incapable of tolerating anything less than hyper-pleasantries – there are many variations of this in-law problem. One way of coping with it may be to demean the child ('Well, perhaps she's the best he deserves', or 'At least she got married before she was twenty-five'), so that the child and his/her spouse can be seen on the same level. Another way is to idealise the child-in-law, and to make sure one is able to do this one may work very hard to see, and to bring out, only good aspects of the child-in-law – or perhaps one works hard not to see anything at all, but to construct according to one's fancy. And however keen the son- or daughter-in-law may initially be to accommodate his/her parents-in-law's needs – thereby protecting him/herself from criticism – the cost may be too high. After a time the claustrophobia becomes stifling. The façade seems to be protecting others from what is unacceptable in oneself. So while one is under the sway of the good behaviour syndrome, one may feel that the whole point of it is to disguise one's own ugliness. In true friendships, or in any relationship involving true contact, people have the opportunity to bring out their fear, their anger, their doubt and test the response and, usually, find that what is hidden is not so awful after all. But the good behaviour syndrome rules this out. One has no chance to prove to others, or to oneself, that there is more than dust and dirt hidden beneath one's polite covers.

Good Relations

'I have a very good relationship with my mother-in-law', Phyllis announced proudly. 'And I have a good relationship with my two daughters-in-law. And my mother was close to her mother-in-law, too.'

Are good and bad relationships between child- and parent-in-law self-perpetuating, in the way they often are between parent and child? Do good parents-in-law produce good children-in-law who can then be good parents-in-law? Do acceptance and appreciation in this difficult area come more easily when one has been accepted and appreciated oneself?

When I asked Phyllis what made her feel close to her mother-in-law she said, 'Well, it's difficult to dislike someone who thinks so highly of me.'

That, I reflected, was only sometimes true. High opinions of someone may be manipulative and placatory: if I think highly of her then she will be persuaded to act out the role of 'such a nice person'. Or the opinion held so favourably might be thoroughly inappropriate, so that one feels it bears little relation to oneself. Why did her mother-in-law think highly of her?

Phyllis was married to a prominent professor of economics who, at the time of their marriage, was a low-paid lecturer. The husband's mother was proud of her son's intellectual achievement and confident – rightly – that it would someday be widely recognised. She approved of Phyllis because she seemed content to live, materially, in a modest fashion. 'I did not crave diamonds or mink', Phyllis explained, 'And I think my mother-in-law thought I was the right person for her son.'

Many people are more prickly than this when it comes to someone's appreciation of them. Not wanting diamonds and mink is a somewhat low requirement for marital compatibility, and being the right person for someone's son leaves one's own identity out of account. But I suppose it is a sufficient reason to be content with one's mother-in-law. Modest expectations are often the key to happiness. Phyllis had towards her daughters-in-law the same attitude she believed her mother-in-law had had towards her: 'They are the right girls for my sons.' The smooth family graph was not without its bumps, however. She added that she had a little trouble with her son-in-law, who came from what she described as a Boston Brahmin family, whereas she was a second- generation Jewish immigrant. But the problem was not that she had difficulty embracing as part of her family someone who had a different background. Her problem was in understanding her daughter's behaviour with her parents-in-law. 'If I were in that position I would be careful about what I said. I would try so hard to fit in. But my daughter insists on saying what she thinks and being herself, and it's not surprising that her husband's parents are disapproving. I would never take such a risk with my husband's family.'

The success of her relationship, then, came down to a version of the good behaviour syndrome. Her mother-in-law might well have said, 'How can I think badly of someone who tried so hard to please me?' The attempt came so naturally that she could not even understand what her own daughter was doing when she insisted on 'being herself' with her parents-in-law. But she knew enough about in-law problems to know that being herself and saying what she thought and not trying hard to fit in would not make the in-laws fond of her daughter. She was admitting, in effect, that the key to good in-law relations is to abandon hope of self-recognition, to tone down self-expression and to practise the good behaviour syndrome.

7
Similarity and Harmony

Do most problems with our in-laws arise because we are different from them, with different family loyalties, different upbringings – perhaps even different cultural and religious and racial backgrounds? If we are like them, or they are like us, do we find it easier to be accepted, and to accept them as family?

Earlier I discussed the theory that people choose marriage partners more on the basis of similarities than on differences, that people try, often unconsciously, to reproduce important aspects of their family of birth. We are not really attracted by opposites but by similarities. We want someone who is able to cope with the same emotions as we, and who must deny or protect him/herself against the same emotions. We tend to choose someone who has reached roughly the same stage of psychological development, or who has had similar problems with a particular stage, so that our partner, like ourself, has trouble dealing with authority, or self-assertion, or independence, or responsibility. We may well be attracted to people who have developed different techniques for dealing with problems, and it therefore seems that we are being attracted to people who have different feelings and attitudes, weaknesses or strengths, but we are really attracted to someone who, in a different way, supports us, reinforces our fears and denials, and protects us from challenges we believe we cannot meet.

We may eventually find that our choice of partner was good, in that the similarities which allowed us to communicate well and to respond deeply and sympathetically to our partner, also allow us to develop around, or even through, our limitations. Or we may have made a poor choice, in that similar fears and deficiencies inhibit growth; one or other partner prevents development and change by putting up a red flag in the face of new ideas or new procedures. Then, there are those partnerships which never had a chance, because the partners were geared to reproduce self-defeating and destructive patterns, and they were adept at choosing someone who would 'help' them do this. Also, one can simply be wrong about another person and marry someone whom one has mistakenly believed to be like oneself, only to discover that the sense of communication and sympathy was based upon fantasy. Such marriages are often referred to as 'mistakes' and tend to be short-lived, whereas even a destructive, violent marriage may not be a mistake, because it gives the partners what they believe they deserve or what they believe they need, and so may be long-lasting and unconsciously fulfilling.

Marital and family therapists have not been able to prove the theory that marriage choice is based largely upon similarity of psychological development, but they do find it the best working hypothesis in therapy. And if the theory is valid, it might well also explain why we resent, or are so easily irritated by, our parents-in-law's differences. We feel they should be like our own parents, but of course they are not. The family history and the family members who contributed to making our spouse like us in many important respects, may well be different from the history and people who made us what we are. So even as we succeed in choosing someone with a similar psychological and emotional make-up, we may be choosing someone whose family is different from ours; and since we may well have trouble with our aim of reproducing our family of birth, or reproducing its best aspects, we may blame these problems on the differences we find in our family of in-laws.

If in fact we do choose a partner from a family very similar to our own, are we less quick to find fault, to be irritated, to be angered by our in-laws? It is very difficult to answer this question, because it is very difficult to assess similarities and differences.

Distinguishing Differences

What is being alike, and what is being different? What qualities or traits matter? Which aspects of upbringing or culture are significant? Any one person or family has some similarities to another, and some differences. How are they measured? Are they ever, or can they be, objectively measured?

Some differences are obvious, such as those of class or race or religion, but even these are more marked, or have far greater significance, in some families than in others. '"Is he Jewish?" is the first question my mother asks me when she hears I have a boyfriend', Rebecca told me. 'It wouldn't matter what else he was – how fine – if he weren't Jewish she would think he was awful. And it wouldn't matter how unsuitable he was in every other respect – if he were Jewish she would approve of him. He could be a real *schlepp*, but if he wore a *yarmulke* she would think he was marvellous.' It was clear that already Rebecca felt trapped by the impersonalisation her parents would bestow upon their son-in-law. He would be defined in terms of his religion, because religion was so important to them.

But parents-in-law do not always take such a clear line in regard to cultural similarities. Sometimes they are just bewildered. 'How on earth am I suppose to talk to a New York Negro?' a white housewife from Minnesota asked me.

No, I don't get on with him – but not because we argue, or because I particularly disapprove. I just don't know what to say to him. And I always think he thinks I don't talk to him easily because I'm a racist. Well, my daughter has married him and I didn't make a fuss and I didn't send her off to Europe when I found out she was dating him, and I didn't threaten to disown her, and if that's not being unprejudiced I don't know what is. I do the best I can, but I'm not going to put on some jazz record when he comes and persuade him to tell me about life in Harlem.

Along with her husband, who said, 'Micky is old enough to make her own decision', the parents-in-law's brusque acceptance seemed like disapproval. Micky herself, however, thought 'they were pretty good about it', and her husband Dave said 'Well, it must be hard for them.' Their tolerance of one another, however, did not make them close, nor did it allow them to see the person beyond the racial difference. 'Grin and bear it' was the most positive response they could muster.

'He's really a nice young man', another white mother-in-law of a West Indian declared.

He cares for my Sue like a good husband. He's not wild, or anything, so I don't have to worry about that. I do worry about the children. I half hope they won't have any, because it would be hard on them, you know, being half and half. But he's a nice young man, and works hard, works for her, just like my Ben worked for his family.

Mrs Potter was clearly trying to look beyond the racial difference, and to assert the presence of important similarities. She was declaring that being 'nice' and working for his family were what counted in a son-in-law, not skin colour. The effort put into seeing things this way was obvious, but none the less worthy for that. But this was how she had to see things if she was going to accept her son-in-law: she had to see him as being 'really' like her own husband.

So the question of 'What differences count?' often becomes

the question of 'What differences will we allow ourselves to count?' In some families a difference of religion or race or nationality or even class plays such an important part in the parents' value-system that a child who marries outside accepted boundaries does indeed seem 'lost', for the family's heritage is then lost within the child, who is therefore seen as a betrayer of the family. This type of 'in-law prejudice' does not necessarily go hand in hand with general prejudices against, say, all non-Jews or all blacks. Rebecca's mother was happy to work alongside Protestants and Catholics. She would willingly hire them, trust them and help them. But she would not have them in her family; she would not tolerate her daughter marrying one, for her family life was Jewish life.

Differences, however, are not always social, cultural, religious or racial differences. Families may have 'differences' in the sense of having quarrels. What, after all, was so different about those two most famous of reluctant in-laws, the Capulets and the Montagues? Their differences involved a history of quarrels, of the type of quarrels that only families within the same class and culture could have engaged in. They created differences to define themselves, to separate themselves when there were no obvious distinguishing factors.

The sum of differences between families is not constant. They can always be manufactured, and often are manufactured in the face of intermarriage. If that nebulous sense of 'belonging to the family' or 'suitable for the family' is lacking in a child-in-law, then the parents-in-law will complain about differences. One area of complaint which is usually kept secret, because parents-in-law feel they should not mention it, is the physical appearance of a child-in-law. It seems wrong, or unfair, to mention whether or not a child-in-law is attractive, though it is obvious that this, along with the dress and manners of a child-in-law, is very important to the parent-in-law's response to a child-in-law. Sometimes a child-in-law's good appearance is so flattering that all objections and suspicions are waylaid. Lisa said:

He was much older than me, and he was Italian, and he was Catholic, but he was so handsome, and so well dressed – my parents had read about Gucci shoes and Longines watches, but they had never seen them before – and they couldn't believe he would make me unhappy. They thought he would be nice because he looked nice. And it took them a long time to see my side of an argument, and to see how trapped I was in his family, with their notions about women.

Indeed, it is very common for parents-in-law to make a thoroughly superficial assessment of a child-in-law. 'How can she love him?' Edna wailed after her first meeting with her daughter's fiancé. 'His hair is greasy. He slouches. And he has a pot belly. Can you imagine? He already has a beer belly. I hate to think what he'll look like ten years from now.' I asked her why she thought her daughter did love him, but she insisted, 'Love him? How can she love him, looking like that? She's smart, I guess. She married him because he's beginning to make a bit of money. And he can play the piano. That's the only good thing about him. He can play the piano pretty well.' (He was in fact a successful concert pianist.)

Superficiality, however, has deep causes. The woman who was so impressed by her son-in-law's appearance that she could not see her daughter's unhappiness, was showing that she undervalued her daughter. Edna, who thought her daughter could not love the pianist because she herself was not attracted to him, was revealing an unwholesome identification with her daughter. She believed that she and her daughter were attracted to the same things, and that if she herself was not attracted to someone then her daughter could not be. The 'difference' she could not accept in her son-in-law was really a difference, a separation, she could not accept between herself and her daughter.

Cross-class Marriage

It is impossible to overestimate the importance to parents of having a child-in-law who seems to 'belong' to the family. The sense that a child-in-law is a stranger, or is fundamentally different, is negative and hostile. We appreciate differences in our friends and even our lovers. We can be excited by them. But parents want their children-in-law to be like them, or like their children, or like some member of their family. Yet in wanting the best for their child, should a parent not sometimes be reasonably pleased by a different child-in-law, a child-in-law who is wealthier, better educated, more influential than the members of their own family? One would expect a parent to be proud that a child has married 'above' his or her family of birth. One might even expect the parent-in-law to idealise a child-in-law, in such cases. But I did not find this. I found cross-class marriage problematic for the parents-in-law.

Parents are almost always proud if their child is more successful than they have been. They have invested so much emotion, time, energy in their child, and identify closely with him or her – not in the sense, necessarily, that they see themselves as the child, but in the sense that they share the child's interests and needs – that the child's success or good fortune is as good as theirs, might as well be theirs. Envy, and the defences which surround envy, have no meaning, because the good fortune belongs to someone who is part of oneself.

If a child marries someone, or marries into a family who is wealthier, more prominent, better educated – or any of the things we count, in considering whether one family is 'better' than another – then the pride may well be mixed, and indeed overpowered by envy and resentment. The parents then feel left out of the success or good fortune, for it is their child's by proxy, and therefore not theirs.

'She's too good for us now', said a mother from Bethnal Green in London. 'They have a big house in Primrose Hill and they drive here in that big German car to get me, and I feel like a freak. The neighbours sometimes stop and stare, and I think they're laughing at me.'

'I expected Mum to be excited about what I had', the daughter Isobel explained.

I kept showing her everything about the new house and all my new clothes. I suppose I was boasting, but I thought she'd be pleased for me. I should have spent more time trying to show her I was still the same. But I thought she would trust me more. I thought she'd trust me to stay the same – certainly towards her, anyway. I try now, because I see how she feels – she's made it very clear! – but I'm getting tired of trying. She always gets shirty with [my husband] because she thinks he's putting her down, but he's not, he's just being normal with her, and speaking to her like he would to anyone else. He's a barrister and he's used to challenging whatever anyone says. She should be able to see that, but she won't. She wants us to treat her like a princess because she thinks I live like a princess. She's upset because we don't look up to her anymore. She's wrong about us looking down at her. Dead wrong. We look straight at her, and that isn't good enough.

The mother's apparent envy of the status her daughter had gained through marriage was not merely an in-law problem, but a problem between parent and child – as indeed so many in-law problems are. What was most important to the mother, however, was the position she believed she had lost in the family. She had been used to seeing herself as breadwinner. Her husband had died some years before, and she had been proud of her strength and her responsibility as she worked for her children, provided them with a stable home and protected them from loneliness and despair. It was difficult for her to see how much she had accomplished, and to accept that part of her job was finished. She could not believe that she could be valued by her daughter when her daughter no longer needed her financial help.

Many parents, considering wealthier in-law families, felt affronted because they had lost their power to help their children and their children's family. They felt they could not give them anything, or that whatever they gave them would be undervalued. 'I'd look after the grandchildren if she wanted me to', said a Philadelphia woman whose son had married the owner of a newspaper for which her own husband had been a printer.

I know she has a lot of social commitments. So I tell her, 'Let me take the kids. I don't live so far away', but she says, 'Oh, don't bother, I have a housekeeper for them.' And when I bring them a little something, like a sweater or skirt, she says, 'Oh, isn't that cute', and just puts it in a drawer and the kids never wear it, and if I bring them a toy they look at it and play with it for five minutes because they have so many toys that nothing is interesting.

If our children marry 'above' us, we may feel we have lost our position in our own family. We may feel smaller, or even redundant. But if our children marry what we may consider to be 'below' us, then we hardly have fewer problems, though they are different problems. In hypogamy (marrying below one's family of birth) as opposed to hypergamy (marrying above one's family of birth), the parents suffer equal resentment and frustration, and again feel that their efforts are useless, but they now seem useless because too little, rather than too much, is realised. 'All the money we spent on her education, and she marries someone who can't support her, so she has to quit graduate school and work in some office. A secretary! And she was going to be a lawyer', one father mused ruefully. 'He could have gone anywhere', a mother boasted of her son.

He was set for the top. You know what I mean. You know my son. He was set to be President. But he married a girl I didn't like. No class. No sense of what you have to give to get something out of this world. So he works hard. She should be glad. But because she doesn't understand what you have to give, she isn't glad. She drinks. Now everyone in Congress knows he has an alcoholic wife. How far will he get now?

Class Fantasies

The crucial point to remember when considering hypergamy and hypogamy is that there seem to be many more cases of the latter, and relatively few of the former. Few parents see a child-in-law as 'better' than their own child, whereas many parents see a child as 'better than' and indeed 'too good for' their child-in-law. Differences in value and class are constructed by one in-law family against another. One family sees itself as different and therefore better, or sees the other as different and therefore worse. Snobbery is so common among in-law families that it may well serve some purpose.

'She's a nice woman for what she is', one mother-in-law said of another. 'She has no profession, of course, no accomplishments, but she tries to convince me how busy she is. She's always rushing around when we visit, but she's not really doing anything, just fussing over this and that. Naturally she feels threatened by me.'

Did the other mother-in-law actually feel threatened by this professional woman's talents? It appears that they were hardly noticed. 'She's very nice', said the second mother-in-law of the first, but then laughed nervously and looked at her husband, who voiced the criticism for her. 'A bit brassy. To say the least', he commented, and then was through with her.

Snobbery between in-law families will escalate if one suspects that the other is in any way, for any reason, critical of the child.

> She [the mother-in-law] thinks he [the son] doesn't treat her [the wife] right. Well, she gets as good as she deserves. She didn't exactly lie on a bed of roses in her home, either. Her parents sent her out to work, made her look after the little ones, because the mother was lazy, or out doing God knows what. She's better off with Rob, I can tell you that. I don't hear *her* [the wife] complain, its only them [the parents-in-law] who rat on the marriage.

114

This was a mother's assessment of her son's parents-in-law's view. The couple themselves did not complain about their in-laws, but one mother-in-law complained about the other, apparently because she believed the in-law family complained about her son – though, as I eventually discovered, the grounds for this belief were in a passing remark, meant as a joke, about whether the wife would have a 'partnership' in the medical degree her husband would earn, because she was supporting him while in medical school.

People are not always reasonable, but their lack of rationality and patience and capacity for forgiveness and tolerance is particularly sparse in regard to their in-laws. To maintain friendships we know we must tolerate a few slights here and there to our vanity, but we are often watchful, waiting for the slight from our in-laws that will allow us to carry a grudge. Surely the passing comment about how the wife had to work to support the husband's studies was no less harmful than those joking complaints one hears from parents about the cost of their children's education. Was the mother nervous because it was the wife, not she or her husband, who was providing for the son's education? Was she not being particularly ungracious and ungrateful?

In-laws change the family balance. A mother-in-law provides a different role for the daughter, say, than does the mother, and so the mother criticises the mother-in-law to maintain herself as the 'best' model. A woman who prides herself on being a good homemaker and mother describes her professionally successful sister-in-law as 'selfish' and 'narrow-minded'. She feels that her sister-in-law's talents are given more weight than hers in the family, and she needs to assert her own value and virtues by citing 'differences' in outlook. Under good circumstances such differences would be tolerated – they would indeed be accepted without a second thought. But in-laws do not tend to create the best circumstances for themselves. They need to assert differences in order to bolster a sense of superiority. By doing this, they hope to establish superior power in regard to the married couple, or perhaps they merely want to maintain some influence, not to lose the regard they had from their child before marriage.

Similarity and Compatibility

In-laws frequently couch their complaints about one another in terms of how they are different from one another; but the question of whether people are alike is different from the question of whether they like one another, or get on with one another. People can be similar, and yet disagree on almost everything. Two people can, for example, be similarly argumentative, or passive, or committed, ambitious, sensitive, volatile. Such similar people may be quick to fall in love, but not to live in harmony. There is no evidence that marriages between 'likes' are more durable or tranquil than marriages between 'unlikes'. Yet there is a prejudice that people with similar interests and similar ideas and similar beliefs will get on better, because they have more in common.

Indeed some problems and heartaches are avoided when people from similar backgrounds, similar cultures, similar races and religions marry. It would be foolish to underestimate the anguish that can be caused by marriages which do not uphold these similarities. A child who marries outside a given religion may, to some parents, truly seem lost to them. If the child, on the other hand, marries someone who endorses the parents' own beliefs and values, then the parents are less likely to feel that the marriage is an insult to them or an act against them. They are more likely to approve of the child-in-law in terms of the marital package he or she provides.

The fact that certain problems are avoided, however, does not mean that there will be fewer or less intense in-law troubles. What does seem to count for a great deal is having the sense that the in-laws 'belong' to one's family. It is this sense of belonging which carries with it the acceptance and trust and willingness to value that families, at their best, reveal. But is similarity at the root of belonging? Does similarity ensure a sense of belonging? Certainly the latter is not the case; and sometimes one looks upon another as belonging to one's family not because the person is similar to any family member but because the person represents precisely what the family lacks. Belonging, like similarity and difference, is a highly subjective assessment.

There is clearly a lack of symmetry as in-laws consider, or care about, similarity and difference. A parent wants his or her child to endorse and exemplify the best, or what the parents regard as the best, in his or her care and teaching and personality. The marriage partner has a tremendous influence on a person's values and life-style and aims and future, so the parent looks to the child-in-law to support the parent's own values, or to enforce what is best in, and best for, the child. A parent will want a child-in-law to be like him- or herself because the child's choice may indicate acceptance of the parent and of the parent's teaching. The child's choice may also reveal rejection of the parent and the parent's teaching, if the spouse is very different from the parent. Being suitable as a child-in-law usually means being like the child, or like the parents, in some obvious respects – race, religion, nationality, income bracket or income prospects, social class. The parent takes a superficial view of the child-in-law. The child, and the parent's views about what the child should be, or what the child needs, come first. A depersonalised view is inherent in the in-law relationship.

Children-in-law, however, do not usually look upon their parents-in-law with the same bias. A spouse usually – but, of course, not always – has the upper hand in terms of influence and loyalty – at least while the marriage lasts. The spouse was chosen. The parents are a given. The parents can think, 'He/she should have married this one, not that one.' The child-in-law cannot so easily imagine away a parent-in-law. Nor does the child-in-law, usually, depend so much upon the external, social features of the parent-in-law. Parents-in-law cannot be dismissed for their religious beliefs, except in so far as they may put pressure upon their child. A spouse cannot look upon his or her parents-in-law as 'not good enough' because they belong to the partner who has been chosen, and the parents-in-law were, presumably, already known. Of course in bad marriages, or in bad patches of marriages, a partner may well feel that he or she had no choice, or had insufficient information to make an appropriate choice, or that he or she simply made a bad choice, and the parents-in-law may become mixed in with all the other complaints and dissatisfactions. But the child-in-law does not approach the parent-in-law with the same *necessary* bias. The parent-in-law looks upon the child-in-law in relation to his or her own child. In a child-in-law, a parent wants what is best for the child, whereas from that same person the spouse seeks what is best for him/herself. There are overlapping interests, because the spouse, too, may want the best for his/her partner. But the initial bias, the different approaches, are difficult to overcome. Hence it helps a great deal if both in-laws have similar ideas about happiness and fulfilment and goodness and success, because then what is wanted from the child-in-law will be what the child-in-law expects, and wants, to give.

Mitigating Differences

It may be cosy and sweet when everyone in the family agrees on what is good for everyone else, but compliance is often too high a price to pay for harmony. People within families feel compelled to assert their individuality – so strongly compelled, in fact, that they bring their differences to the fore, even when there is no need to do so. However similar families of in-laws are, there will always be some differences, some grounds for clashes and, it seems, in-laws are as ready as adolescents to throw their differences in one another's faces, challenging one another with their separateness, with their opposition.

A professor at London University, Mark, had married a Cambridge don, Alice, whose family of birth was very similar to his. Both partners had been brought up in middle-class homes, with parents highly ambitious for the intellectual achievements of their children; both children had satisfied their parents in this respect. Both sets of parents, however, were now also defensive in face of their children's accomplishments, and sought to 'keep their own end up'. They did this by loudly proclaiming the prejudices – or, from their point of view, beliefs – which they knew would be most abhorred by the child-in-law. Alice's father would announce, within one hour of every visit, that Mark, his son-in-law, knew nothing about the conspiracy of the blacks, and that his liberalism was based on ignorance and soft-mindedness. Mark's father, in turn, would rile his daughter-in-law with anti-Semitic remarks (she was half Jewish) which were gratuitous and, of course, insulting. Each father-in-law knew best how to get himself 'noticed' and to ruffle the composure and certainty of the child-in-law. It appeared that harmony threatened them with assimilation, and that they would rather appear pigheaded and crude than have their individuality and separateness ignored.

'Jack can go weeks without discussing politics with me', Emma said of her husband, 'but I can't trust him for five minutes with my parents.' She begged him not to bring up politics as they set off for a three-day visit at her parents' home in North Carolina. She came from a family of Southern Democrats, that is, people who are Democrats simply because they would never support the Republican party to which Lincoln had belonged, not because the body or their beliefs or sympathies are in keeping with those of the present Democratic party. Jack, on the other hand, was a staunch liberal Democrat, who disagreed with and disapproved of every political, social or economic statement uttered by his father-in-law.

The first day of their visit went smoothly. Both husband and father-in-law had been primed by their wives not to discuss difficult issues. On the following day, at lunch, they were suddenly at loggerheads. 'I don't know why it happened', Emma said afterwards.

No one wanted it to happen, but everyone could see it starting and no one could stop it. My mother and I kept on breaking in and saying stupid things like 'What a lovely meal', but they just glared at us. Jack said my Dad was goading him on, but it was six of one and half a dozen of the other. Jack just wouldn't let any comment pass him by, and my Dad knew this, but he played the innocent and said, as though he wasn't talking to anyone in particular, 'How about that? Edward Kennedy is trying to play the saint. I guess he knows as much about Ethiopia as he does about Ireland', and Jack went wild, as my Dad knew he would, and started on at him about how people suspected motives when they couldn't justify any criticism of what the person was doing, and the argument deteriorated from there, and they were finally hurling terms like 'bigot' at one another, and it was all I could do not to cry. I thought my folks would be real proud of Jack, because he's just what they always said they wanted in a son-in-law. He's smart. He's successful – or certainly will be – and he's good-looking and he's nice. He couldn't be more suitable, and yet they're always fighting.

Of course, the fights were not simply about politics. The father's and son-in-law's political differences became an issue because they were trying to establish other differences. The father wanted to diminish the son-in-law a little in his daughter's eyes, and the son-in-law felt compelled to 'keep his own up' in face of this challenge. They used these relatively minor differences to establish themselves as opposites. After they had burned out the political argument, the family sat in sullen silence until the mother-in-law began to talk about things she knew they agreed on – such as how to mend a leaking roof and what type of money-market fund gave the best value. The two men accepted the reconciliation thrust upon them by the mother-in-law, a reconciliation based upon points of agreement.

Sex Differences

Similarities, like differences, must be created or granted significance. It is not enough that they simply exist. If similarities are to be important, then in-laws must agree on their importance, or lend relatively insignificant things importance simply because they do provide points of agreement. Fathers and sons-in-law tend to argue when they hold different political and social views. Daughters-in-law and the spouse's parents do not actually agree more often about political and social matters, but they argue about them less, are better at talking about other things. Clashes between daughters-in-law and mothers tend to be within the domestic arena, about how to load up the refrigerator or how long to cook the roast. When they make an effort to get on, they tend to swap tips about sewing and cleaning – though some young women today resent this kind of conversation because it presupposes a role they find limiting or even stifling. Therefore the mother-in-law may be thrown by the fact that certain topics cause irritation, and may be at a loss to know what to talk about, or even to understand how or why she has caused offence.

Generally, people must agree on what they will argue about. They often agree, too, on what the issues behind the argument are. The son-in-law and father who fought about politics each knew that self-esteem and the daughter's/wife's esteem were at stake. When issues like these are not involved, then the ostensible differences can be passed over, and they do not stimulate a battle. Men and women, as in-laws, seem to argue about different things not because men and women hold a different range of views, but because as in-laws they confront one another in set ways. Few people feel they have escaped sexual stereotypes when they confront their in-laws. It is part of the depersonalisation inherent in the relationship.

Belonging

Does it really matter whether in-laws have anything in common, or whether they are alike? Husband and wife must have enough in common to form one household and one family unit, but in-laws normally form a different household and a different unit. There is no necessity for broad areas of agreement, or for the general similarities that often lead to agreement. Yet their differences can so easily irritate us, hurt us or enrage us.

121

The problem is that however different, however separate from us our in-laws are in terms of character, upbringing or appearance, they have become family, in law. We judge them and feel comfortable or uncomfortable with them accordingly. We may be projecting family feelings upon them, and be resentful when the projection fails – or we may be resentful, too, when the projection takes, but they somehow disappoint or injure us as family. Sometimes we may feel liberated by an in-law's difference from our own family. Our parents-in-law, for example, may exhibit a more open system, in which greater variety and intensity of feeling and opinions are tolerated. A son- or daughter-in-law may provide us with the appreciation, or the achievement, we regret not finding in our own child. But even these differences are embraced because they belong to, or are exhibited by, a family member.

Many people say that they get on with an in-law because they have much in common – or that they don't get on because they have very little in common. The trouble here is that the assessment of similarities and differences is highly subjective. The assessment itself is based on a sense of belonging, which is itself far more complex than conscious agreement or common interests. People see themselves as similar when they approve of one another, when they flatter one another's self-image; whereas two people anyone else would think of as similar may consider themselves different because each challenges the other in some uncomfortable way. In-laws who get on because they have a great deal in common actually find a great deal in common because they get on; and in-laws who look upon one another as different may be looking at an unwelcome mirror image of many of their own features. Similarities and differences in themselves have little relation to harmony or disjunction.

8
Living In/Moving Out

Now, take my mother-in-law. She's all right. Not the usual type. Don't mind having her round a bit. Always knocks before she comes in. To our bedroom. On Sunday morning. Gives us a cup of tea, too. Nothing like a cup of tea to help start the day. (*pause*) But four in the morning's a bit early on Sunday. 'Angie', she shrieks, 'you've got two backs!'

The comedian's routine about the mother-in-law is wearisomely familiar. She intrudes on the couple's sex life, mostly by ignoring that they have a sex life. She criticises the son-in-law to her daughter and to her grandchildren. She despises the son-in-law's parents, whom she criticises in front of the son-in-law. She causes contention between the couple with her interference, and then blames the son-in-law for being quarrelsome. The son-in-law can't wait to get her out of the house, and she can't wait to get her daughter away from her son-in-law.

The hostility towards the mother-in-law is a very old part of our culture, and found in all classes of our society, but this type of music-hall derision, so similar to the compulsory joking found in other societies, arose particularly among the working class because of the special dependence foisted upon the son-in-law. 'I married her – not her bleeding mother', a man might insist; and indeed, if at all possible, the couple find their own home, rather than live with one of the partner's parents. However, this is not always possible. Housing shortages, especially in the 1940s and 1950s, often made it necessary for the couple to remain in a parent's home. As the lesser of two evils, the couple usually lived with the wife's parents, and from this arose the intense fuel for the typical mother-in-law joke.

The modern version of the extended family (two or more generations of married couples living under one roof) emerged in a fascinating study of families in east London.[1] The young couple who had no chance of financing or finding their own home, would stay with the wife's parents because at least the women, who were after all more bound to the home, had a chance of getting along. One had taught the other what she knew about domestic matters, so their approach to household tasks was likely to be the same. When the couple had to live with the husband's parents there was usually tremendous tension between the daughter-in-law and mother-in-law. First there were conflicts about simple domestic matters, whether the washing should be done on Monday or Tuesday, whether the steps had or had not been sufficiently scrubbed, what was the best use of certain rationed food. Underlying these disagreements were rivalries about dominance in the home and about who was closer to the son/husband. The husband's mother is accustomed to being dominant in her home. She has looked after her son all his life, and believes she knows best how to make him comfortable and happy. Why should she change her ways, why should she step back, just because a daughter-in-law has come to live with her? One mother-in-law who was visiting her son and daughter-in-law after they had been able to set up a home of their own, used to answer the phone (she had never had one!) and insist that she was Mrs Askew, when the caller asked to speak to her son's wife. In this way she persisted in denying that her daughter-in-law had any claim to the same name, or to be 'the woman of the house'. For the young wife, however, change seems reasonable, and as a wife she wants to be dominant and be the primary influence on her husband. In-laws living under the same roof have many ways of denying one another, or negating the other's importance. A woman who did live with her mother-in-law practised something like strict avoidance, except that the silence between them registered hostility rather than prevented it. 'I've got two rooms with my mother-in-law', she explained. 'I have to go down three flights for every drop of water, and as soon as I come into her kitchen, she turns her back. We never speak to each other even if we meet in the street.'[2]

If there is tension between a spouse and a parent-in-law, then the marriage itself tends to be stormy. Both partners have an interest in minimising conflict with any parent-in-law, and in fact open conflict is rare, probably because it would be so painful for everyone. The husband would consent to live with his wife's parents rather than with his own, even though he might be more comfortable with his own, because he knew that if his wife had problems with her in-laws then he would have trouble with her. Yet often the husband, when he lived with his parents-in-law, felt as though he was facing a triangle in his marriage. The young wife was usually very attached to her mother, and even if she was not living with her, would live nearby, and could spend several hours with her each day. The husband had to live with or near the mother-in-law because his wife wanted to preserve this closeness. In any argument the husband felt that his loyalty must be towards his wife, but his wife always felt that she must side with her mother – so that the husband had no one to support him. As a defence he practised a limited form of avoidance, which he could do without indicating the hostility which avoidance between daughter-in-law and mother-in-law must suggest. He simply kept a 'low profile' – which, on domestic territory, a man can do more easily than a woman – and would spend evenings out with his mates, or at the pub. The women benefited enormously from the closeness of their mothers – who participated in childcare – but the son-in-law in an extended family (and even if the couple were not living under the same roof as the parents-in-law, there could be a sense of extended family in the amount of time the wife spent with her mother) would have liked to get as far away from his mother-in-law as possible, even if he claimed to have 'nothing against her'.[3]

The derision of the mother-in-law arose from her power, not only her power in the home but also her power over her daughter. The weaker the husband became, the greater was his dependence on the wife and mother-in-law, and the stronger was the alliance between the women. Insecurity and kinship seem inextricably bound together. When a husband is out of work, the wife will turn to her own family for help, and the husband's position is undermined further. He tends to feel excluded and resentful. As the wife/mother-in-law alliance takes charge of the home and the children, he withdraws further, and finds support from friends or lovers. Social workers in Bethnal Green certainly blamed many divorces upon 'Mum's sometimes far from benign influence',[4] in that the help she gave made the unemployed husband redundant in his own family too. Because he was out of work, he was seen by the parents-in-law as vagrant and unreliable.

Among the families of unemployed today, I found the same reliance on the wife's family, but by and large there was sympathy for the unemployed son-in-law. The wife's parents tended to see him as a victim of the financial situation rather than as lazy or unreliable. None the less, the help they offered sometimes had a negative affect on the husband. They would offer help with the children, so that the wife could increase her hours of work or begin to market a previously developed skill. This in effect prevented the unemployed husband from developing domestic skills himself, which might have strengthened his position in the home. The mother-in-law, as she helped with childcare, tended to think that the father's position should be 'out looking for work', even in areas in which there was so little change from day to day and so few openings that job-searching could not reasonably be done full time. The mother-in-law therefore preserved sex-typed roles, which gave her a position of importance in the unemployed son-in-law's home and prevented him from becoming a more positive force in his family.

Among the striking miners, the clashes between in-laws, if they held different beliefs from their sons-in-law about whether or not to continue the strike, were as fiery as between Irish in-laws holding different political or religious views. In many cases the 'differences of opinion' caused rifts which may never heal. The wife usually sided with her husband, even though she had reservations, and she wanted her parents to stay out of it. ('But no', a mother of three children told me, 'they had to have their say every time they saw [my husband].') These arguments initially appeared to threaten the principle that a wife's parents will help out in times of difficulty, and the wife had actually told her parents that if 'they kept on at Jim' they would have to stay out of their lives. The next day, however, her mother was back to visit 'bringing two dozen eggs and a sorry smile' and the two women did not mention the previous day's quarrel, but the son-in-law 'slipped out the back door when he heard her voice'. The son-in-law's avoidance preserved harmony but diminished his position in the home. The wife/mother-in-law alliance was too strong to break. Often, the son-in-law's only retaliation is through mother-in-law jokes, which both acknowledge and deprecate her power.

Bereft In-Laws

When elderly people lose their husbands or wives most of them continue to live in their own home, now alone. Do their children and children-in-law neglect them? Are they unwanted? Are they condemned to loneliness because the younger married couple rejects them?

The truth is that most old people want to preserve their independence. If they left their own home to join that of a son or daughter they would lose their right to run the home in their own way, to entertain friends as they wished and to make their own day-to-day decisions. One woman laughed at the notion of staying in her son and daughter-in-law's home. 'Imagine my coming in late and them asking me where I've been.' She slapped the table and snorted. Another woman thought that if she lived with her daughter and grandchildren then she would have to help out in the home, to pay for her keep. 'I could never say "no" if they asked me to stay with the children. I could never let on that I had another engagement. I'd be thinking all the time that I had to help out, because they were letting me live there. Maybe I'd get used to it, but I don't think so.'

These people did not particularly like being alone. As a rule they missed their partner greatly, and were glad of any company. They wanted to visit their children and grandchildren, but they only chose to live with them if independence was already ruled out by physical or mental infirmity. And even the widow or widower would usually respect the privacy of a child's marriage, and choose to live with an unmarried son or daughter rather than a married one. Of course there are grieving, aging people who use their weakness as a weapon against the younger generation, and who try to worm their way into the family home by loading guilt upon the son or daughter ('I devoted my life to you and now I'm alone'), and perhaps even try to come between the child and his or her spouse by insisting that obligations to a parent override those to a husband or wife. But in face of this stereotype in-law, which is the unhappy exception rather than the rule, most lonely, elderly people put up fierce resistance. They would like to live near at least one child, and may spend many hours a day in the child's home (usually it is a daughter), but they make themselves scarce rather than interfere. One widow explained why she did not want to live in her daughter's home, and why she 'laid low' when the son-in-law was about: the husband and wife may 'have a cross word and you get to thinking about it and perhaps you can't keep quiet'.[5]

The reserve and respect widows and widowers showed

towards their children's marriages were certainly enforced by a wish to avoid being identified as the typical interfering in-law. Without the support of the spouse, they seemed far more sensitive to criticism from a son- or daughter-in-law, and their own complaints about a child-in-law shifted from complaints about what the son- or daughter-in-law did, how he or she behaved towards the spouse and grandchildren, to complaints about his or her attitude towards him/herself. Sometimes they felt their sons-in-law were contemptuous of them, or that their daughters-in-law would 'not listen to a word I say'. They were touchy about a son- or daughter-in-law interfering in their own child's affection. Some widows thought that if their sons 'made a fuss' of them the wives would be annoyed and 'get a bit catty'.[6]

The son- or daughter-in-law, however, tended to see him/herself as less critical – or less openly critical – of the parent-in-law as a widow or widower. They acknowledged the claim of loyalty a grieving parent had on his or her own child, and usually made it possible for the spouse to go some way towards honouring that claim. Again, there were exceptions, such as the wife who told her husband that he could choose between having her in the house or his mother – that he could not have both. Frequently, though, the parent-in-law who had lost a spouse was less of a threat to the son- or daughter-in-law because the parent-in-law was seen to be less powerful. The parents-in-law could no longer form a coalition against the son- or daughter-in-law, working together to assign roles or control behaviour. Also, the widow or widower had less authority, and perhaps less desire, to maintain domestic control. He or she was willing to let the son- or daughter-in-law have his or her say, and to fit in as a guest, rather than run the home. When two generations had been living together, but leading separate domestic lives (with separate kitchens and eating areas), it was common for the parent-in-law, at the death of his/her spouse, to become incorporated in the younger generation.[7] What may also make things easier for the son- or daughter-in-law is that he/she now has a clearly defined role as helper or comforter – and that is an easier role to assume than that of receiver, the one in debt, the one who has no responsibility and who has given up nothing, has made no proof of generosity. The parent-in-law is usually sensitive to this shift of moral cachet, and tries to prevent the younger couple from being too obviously noble, but the younger couple seldom notice these efforts. 'We're glad to be of help, now that she's alone', they often said. 'We let her do things around the house. She likes to think she's being useful.'

The picture was very different when a son or daughter died, leaving the son- or daughter-in-law as widower or widow. I expected to find, almost uniformly, a bond based on grief. Sometimes this did occur. The son- or daughter-in-law was the strongest living tie the parents-in-law had with their dead child. In many cases this bond persisted throughout the son- or daughter-in-law's remarriage, and the interest in the son- or daughter-in-law's children by the new spouse was as close as anything could be to a grandparent's interest. But, like all in-law stories, many revealed disturbing gaps in human sympathy and our capacity for forgiveness.

The hostility between in-laws often appears so petty and superficial that one might expect these battles to become irrelevant in the face of something as profound as grief, but in fact poor relations among in-laws tended to break down totally under mutual recriminations. The child's death is unexpected, and cannot be accepted in the way that the death of an elderly parent-in-law usually can be. When a younger person dies, the parent says it was the spouse's fault – 'She drove him too hard', or 'If he had really cared, he would have seen she was ailing.' Since grief is so closely bound up with guilt anyway, these unanswerable charges are unforgivable. How can one be sure that they aren't true? Yet what good do they do, and what can one do to make reparation if they do carry some truth? In the shock of grief, irrationality has its day. There is less incentive to hold back one's thoughts and feelings – all may seem lost whatever we do. Past resentments, which have hitherto been contained, become the hook on which to hang many troubles. As in primitive societies, wherein misfortune is thought to be the realisation of someone's displeasure, the outsider is the first under suspicion, especially an outsider within the family – that is, an in-law. Also, there is less meaning, after the death of the child who married the outsider, to the family connection, and therefore less willingness to tolerate faults or suspected faults in the in-law. The 'gamblers' or 'spongers' or 'gossips' who were accepted for the sake of the spouse are outcasts now that the spouse is dead.

Sometimes the resentment is directed against the parents-in-law. 'They did nothing for him when he was alive', one widow said, 'why should they bother now?' Envy, too, could poison a relationship between a widow and a brother- or sister-in-law, because she could not accept another's happiness, or because contact with a spouse's relatives revived grief. One widow said that she tried to avoid her brother-in-law because he was so like her husband that when she saw him it kept 'bringing back memories'.[8]

Behaviour, however, is often better than feeling, and most in-laws, however bitter, acknowledged one another the courtesy of at least an occasional visit, and few grandparents, as the result of the death of their child, were denied, or sought to avoid, contact with their grandchildren. Yet there were seldom more frequent visits between in-laws as the result of a spouse's death.[9] The widow or widower sought support mainly from his or her own family – as ever, it was blood kinship that held fast through adversity.

House Divided – In-Laws and Divorce

In-laws are given to us with marriage, but are they taken away with the dissolution of marriage? If, as they say, blood is thicker than water, and if in-law relationships, as they seem to be, are so often constituted by poisoned water, does divorce not offer the opportunity to be free of unwanted in-laws, along with an unwanted spouse? The fact that stories about in-laws and divorce are rarely so cut and dried indicates that these troublesome waters do become mixed with blood, for better and for worse.

Divorce is a procedure with many stages, sometimes quite separate, sometimes overlapping and interlocked. In the emotional stage which precedes divorce, one or both partners come to find the continuation of the marriage intolerable. Then follow legal and financial matters, combined with issues of childcare and domestic arrangements. Parents-in-law can stand behind their child and goad him or her into vindictiveness (often an easy thing to do during divorce) and offer their support in terms of money or knowledge or energy. Many divorcing people want their parents to stay out of their affairs; because their emotions have already been so heavily taxed, they do not want to be pushed, or to push further. But divorce can stimulate the fighting spirit in otherwise reasonable and fair people, and with their family behind them, they can seem quite content to ruin their ex-spouse – either financially or humanly, by taking away their children or denying them access to the children.

Another stage in divorce involves an adaptation to one's new status as a single person, and perhaps as a single parent. Each partner has to accustom him/herself to a new social status and a new marital identity. Relatives and in-laws will do what they can to confuse the already complicated situation. If they show support for the ex-partner then they will arouse anxiety, because the hostility towards one's previous mate is seldom without ambivalence. If they attack the ex-spouse, they will perhaps help confirm feelings of separation from the former partner, but they will also leave one confused as to the meaning of the marriage – for even when the marriage has ended, the partners need to make some sense of it. The typical and expected pattern is for the parents to rally around their child, and for the in-laws to attack the child's spouse, admitting that they never really liked him/her, or adding a helpful 'I told you so.'

The parents and parents-in-law of the divorcing couple are often as confused as the couple themselves, and they may present the typical image on one day and a very different one the next. Sometimes the parents-in-law feel utterly disillusioned when their child makes certain revelations about the marriage and, like all sudden changes of view, it may be denied fifteen minutes after it has hit one in the face. Sometimes the parents persist in wanting their child's marriage to continue, and so they swallow their criticisms as they try to pave the way for reconciliation. Ruth-Ann's family were appalled when they learned of her husband's infidelities, and claimed that their view of him was utterly changed – they seemed to feel as betrayed as she – but a few days later they were offering to pay for marital therapy, hoping that somehow their previous image of the 'good' son-in-law could be reinstated. In her distress at the discovery that she had lost her husband to another woman, Ruth-Ann was naturally highly irritable. Her parents tried to persuade her to control her temper. 'No wonder he wants another woman. All you do is scream and cry', her father told her. Quite unreasonably they blamed her – seeing the behaviour which arose from her husband's infidelity as its cause. Many parents counter their children's complaints about their spouses with criticisms of them. 'You're no angel either', or 'It's give and take in a marriage. How much do you give him/her?'

A parent's fears and misgivings about a child may emerge in attitudes towards a child-in-law, who is admired because the child loves him/her, who is denigrated for the same reason, who is held to be valuable because he/she deigned to marry one's less than beautiful child, who must be praised because somehow he/she manages to put up with one's child's quirks and failings. If a child-in-law fulfils, on behalf of the parent-in-law, some ambition, then the child really gets a rough deal in times of marital conflict. Judy laughingly explained that she had never had anyone to go to with her marriage problems. 'My mother is warm and loving, but there is no way she is going to see that this successful doctor is anything less than perfect.' Such idealisation of children-in-law is very difficult to forgo. On the whole, it seemed easier to find fault with one's child.

The shift of loyalties demanded of relatives during a divorce may well stand a natural relationship on its head as the in-law becomes the favoured one and the blood relative becomes the outcast. Ruth-Ann's parents were offering her support, even as they spoke up for their son-in-law, but the son-in-law's parents actually cast him out. As usual, the story behind this distribution of loyalties is hardly simple, and has little to do with fairness. Here the explanation spans at least two generations.

The husband's mother's father had left his family to seek his fortune in Australia. The official story was that he would return, or send for his family, when a reasonable fortune was made. He never returned, and he never sent for his family. The daughter (the husband's mother), however, believed the official story that he had died in an unfortunate accident while building the farm that was to be the family home. The father had indeed died, and it is impossible to know what he would have done had he lived, but in the three years he was in Australia he married again, commiting bigamy, and fathered a child by his Australian 'wife'. Years later, and just before her son's divorce, the daughter met her father's Australian child, and therefore faced incontrovertible proof that he had not been faithful to his English family. The fantasy she had harboured for most of her life of a loving father was crushed – and the effect was all the more crushing because she had probably known the truth all along. When her son abandoned his wife for another woman, she identified with her daughter-in-law, who was abandoned as she had been abandoned by her father at fourteen. Moreover, she turned against her son because he was the betrayer – like her father, like his grandfather. She cast out her son because he represented the cruel betrayal of her childhood, which she could no longer tolerate, now that she had lost the fantasy of her father's love.

Support Systems

Whom we side with has a great deal to do with our own needs and fantasies, and very little to do with a straightforward sense of justice and desserts. The attachments and associations that make one person an 'insider' and another an outcast usually have a less than obvious history. Habit may prove to be thicker than either blood or water, as may need. In poorer black families in America there is a particularly close kin system offering wide-ranging support – from shelter for an abandoned or beaten mother to a few dollars for an unpaid grocery bill.[10] 'In-law' relationships arise even when a partnership is unconfirmed by marriage, and the in-law relationship may be untouched by separation (which is not as commonly followed by divorce as it is among white middle-class couples, since divorce involves expense and some contact with the legal system). The mother-in-law may continue looking after her grandchildren whatever her son's position in her daughter-in-law's home. She is the grandmother, and the daughter-in-law's work helps support her grandchildren, and so she will help her daughter-in-law continue to work by caring for the children during the day. Or perhaps she expects her son to behave like her husband or father, and believes that only women will stand by their families, and so solidarity among the women takes precedence over loyalty to the son.

Sometimes the in-laws will try to compensate for a slight delivered by a son or daughter. The parents will feel guilty on their child's behalf, and so try to minimise the loneliness of an abandoned spouse. Or the spouse may have established a role within the in-law family which refuses to be dissolved by the dissolution of the marriage. Alice had been married to Peter for fifteen years when he left her. They had no children, but she was closely involved with her nephews and nieces who lived nearby. At family gatherings, her former in-laws would always include her – and this made her former husband stay away, since meetings with Alice were now uncomfortable. As a single woman with no children, her former in-laws often turned to her when they needed family aid, just as one might turn to a healthy maiden aunt. When Peter's brother's wife died suddenly, Alice was called upon to help him out. She did so as a family member, but since she was no longer actually family, it was easy for a romantic attachment to develop. Eventually she became sister-in-law to her former husband and to her husband's current wife. The support system had again turned her in to a bona fide member of the family.

Do In-Laws Cause Divorce?

In-laws can play a wide variety of roles in the processes of divorce, but do they, in our society, ever cause it? Many marital quarrels concern in-laws, and quarrels among in-laws can make a marriage stormy, but in truly bad marriages, the quarrels, even if they seem to be about in-laws, are usually about the marriage, or the marriage partners and their children, not about in-laws – except in so far as in-laws represent us and become part of us, or part of our marriage partner. I have already shown how parents become part of us and how in-laws can become part of our marriage (Chapter 4: 'My Spouse, My Self'), and how we may use complaints against in-laws to help our marriage, either by taking on our spouse's battles of separation or by attributing all our spouse's faults to our parents-in-law, thus splitting off faults from our partner, even while we know they are there. It is also clear that these attempted solutions to certain marital difficulties may fail, and be fed back into marital tension, as when the husband sees his wife's hostility towards his mother as intolerable – because she is expressing the hostility on his behalf, and this has become her task because he cannot admit his own hostility, although her task is fruitless because he cannot tolerate it in her either.

Quarrels about-in laws, or quarrels with in-laws that seem to destroy a marriage, are never just about or between in-laws. In Edward Albee's play, *Who's Afraid of Virginia Woolf?*, the warring couple George and Martha keep Martha's father close at hand for reference in their battles (George is in the history department, unlike 'Daddy' who *was* the history department), but the husband's failure to live up to his wife's ideal – an ideal formed by her image of her father – is part of their coalition, their agreement to demean one another in order to deny their need for one another. The expressed disappointment is clearly a ruse to avoid – in Martha's case – self-denigration. In George's case, he accepts accusations of academic failure in order to avoid more personal and painful disappointments of childlessness, and the inability to admit to

136

his own childlike needs of dependence and attachment, which all healthy adults have.

I could find no cases of marital conflict involving in-laws, and leading to marital breakdown, which did not prove to be about something else, about something within the partners themselves, and within the marriage itself. Was the following marital story an exception?

The first five sessions with a marital therapist, who was helping a working-class family in West Berlin, were devoted to the couple's discussion of visits they routinely made to the husband's parents in East Berlin.[11] The husband/son saw himself as a representative of the more lucrative West. It was not simply a matter of pride, of wanting to show how well he was doing (though in fact he was not well off), but also a matter of fulfilling his parents' expectations. They knew that he had access to greater material wealth, but had no understanding of its limits. The wife resented the expense both of the visits and the gifts, which she saw as ruining the family – for the toll was not only financial, but moral and social as well, since (the wife believed, though this was not proven) the husband had persuaded their son to steal some particularly status-giving presents. The accusations and counter-accusations in the sessions seemed to centre around divided loyalties – who came first? who would be cared for first? how far would the husband go in neglecting his wife and children to provide for his parents, or to protect their image of him, to protect them from seeing how cruel were their demands on and expectations of their son? The husband countered that the wife had no family feeling and no imagination, in that she refused to understand how she would feel in his position, or in his parents' position, and that she was really more interested in her own selfish comforts than in the well-being of the family. He saw himself as trying to make good in a new, expanding culture, but having ties to an older, more backward culture – or, as he put it, he had two sets of responsibilities, and was getting no support from his wife, who didn't want to share anything. She didn't understand how much he owed his parents, how dreary their lives would be without the gifts, and

137

how little, really, it took from their family – but then (contradictions are very common in these situations) he claimed the younger family should be willing to make sacrifices for the older family, because the older family only had hope through the younger.

Gradually it became clear that the husband resented the present-giving and the frequent visits, too, but what enraged him about his wife's attitude was not merely that it confronted what he could not admit, but also that it prodded him towards admitting the guilt which bound him to his parents and made him, compulsively, attempt some compensation through his gifts. For his bonds to his family had a history of incest, which he had briefly engaged in with his older sister, and which had convinced him of what his wife was so loudly saying now – that there was a conflict between his loyalty to his family of birth and his marriage. The fights between him and his wife occurred regularly after a visit to his family, and the severity of the fight was in direct proportion to the value of the presents given, but the issue was not simply the wife's objection to the expense, but also his own disappointment that these costly gifts were not sufficient to assuage his guilt – which was double-edged guilt at living apart from the family to which he was so closely bound (through incest) and, simultaneously, at having been so closely bound to the family that his sexual relations with his wife, or any outsider, were somehow polluted, a sign of family disloyalty.

In-laws may want to destroy their relative's marriage, even when they believe they don't. Possessiveness and resentment are all too clearly expressed in their behaviour. But the harm they may do to a marriage is indirect and incalculable. It is harm done to their relative's capacity for attachment or for what we call free choice in marriage, which is really the ability to make a choice that is not going to defeat us. In-laws, then, are no worse and no better than our own parents, who play the same part in our marriage. We simply see more clearly the faults of our in-laws and, as adults, resent them just as we resented our parents' faults when we were adolescents. In-laws are part of the family, after all.

9
The Birth of Grandparents

A grandchild provides many opportunities for consolidation and reconciliation within a family. Children who have had poor relationships with their own parents may, when they become parents themselves, offer their children as a reparative gift. Where they feel they could not provide sufficient satisfaction, or overcome tension, their children, who are part of themselves, may do so. Parents-in-law, too, are often forgiven for past sins. 'I understand how important families are', a young mother said as she held her son. 'When my child grows up I will want to have contact with him and his wife.' Some mothers of sons claim that they now understand how difficult it is for the mother to step aside as the most important woman in a child's life. Some sons- and daughters-in-law feel less threatened by the parents-in-law now that they are parents themselves, and become more tolerant. In turn, the parents-in-law may see them less as an outsider, now they have parented a family member, or they may be offered a new respect and appreciation for attaining the status of parent.

139

Grandparents, too, are offered a new chance with childcare or child involvement – and this second chance is easier than the first. Grandparents can accept individuality in their grandchildren more easily than in their children, upon whom they are likely to thrust their own hopes and needs. Self-doubt does not interfere so often with the relationship between grandparent and grandchild, since the grandparent does not blame him/herself for the child's shortcomings, failures and mistakes. Strict, forbidding parents often make lenient, warm grandparents. It is not the grandparents' task to socialise the child. They tend to be unconcerned with discipline, and to adopt the child's point of view – sometimes in opposition to the parents. Whereas in most healthy families there is a clear crossgenerational hierarchy between parents and children – with authority and protective care on the one side, and dependence, along with a certain amount of respect and obedience, on the other, between grandparents and grandchildren there is a greater degree of equality.[1]

Normal changes in family roles, however, do not always come without a struggle, or without attempts by one or more members to retain a previous status and its accompanying perks. Cross-generational roles should change with the birth of grandchildren, with the new parents now having greater authority and the older couple taking a back seat even when they disagree. But this is not always easy. If the new parents are very young or anxious, or if one of them has maintained a dependent relationship with his or her parents, the new grandparents will be unable to trust the new parents with the child. One grandmother, who virtually mothered two generations – her daughter and her daughter's children – was quite adept at preventing her son-in-law, or any prospective son-in-law, from taking an active paternal role, probably because she did not want to lose her influence or usefulness, or because she had seen her own daughter delegate parental responsibility and expected all her peers to do the same. Sometimes the grandparent – usually the maternal grandmother – acquires and maintains a parental position because her daughter lacks a husband's support. One new father saw his wife and mother-in-law forming an alliance in the care of the baby, and he recognised that his wife needed her mother's help since he worked long hours and at some distance from home. He changed jobs, and spent more time at home, but the wife's resentment at having been 'abandoned' (or so it seemed to her) when their child was born, and the grandmother's attachment to the infant, created a barrier between him and the child. From his point of view he had acted as fairly and responsibly as possible, giving up his job as soon as he realised its domestic implications – and taking another job which allowed him to spend time at home. But the wife/mother-in-law coalition defeated his best efforts.

But power and control are hardly the only issues. The grandparents care profoundly about their grandchildren. Their sense of what is good for them is bound up with their own values and their own culture. Differences of religion,which may have been in the background, may emerge as the grandparent fights to preserve what he or she sees as the child's salvation. Elizabeth held a secret christening ceremony for her first grandson, and when her daughter and son-in-law discovered this, they were outraged. 'It can't do any harm', she reasoned, yet from the parents' point of view it was an insult to their decision. 'You're not going to circumcise him, are you?' Paul demanded of his Jewish daughter-in-law. A television series on Jews in America was fresh in his mind, with the cruelty of the *Bris* ceremony exposed. 'Of course I am', she answered, 'anyone with any Jewish identity would have her son circumcised.' The Protestant mother-in-law could not let this pass, but pleaded in private with her son to 'show the woman some reason'. To them, circumcision involved maiming. It seemed barbaric and unnecessary.

Marriages between people of similar cultures may be easier if only because it is easier for the parents-in-law, especially when they become grandparents. 'I wouldn't dream of interfering . . .' invariably precedes or concludes marked interference. But how can they refrain, when they care so deeply about the grandchild's well-being? Sally could accept her daughter's marriage to someone who voted Labour, but very early on she tried to avoid what seemed to her as a crime against her grandchildren – their education at a state school. At every birthday and holiday she announced, 'I'm not giving them a present, I'm just setting aside twenty-five more pounds in their school fund. Just in case you change your mind', she added as her son-in-law began to protest. 'I want them to have it just in case. I'm not telling you what to do.'

The Baby Grenade

The birth of a child changes the balance of the marriage. Previously it was a relationship primarily between the husband and the wife. The new arrival may threaten the special intimacy. So much is now demanded of the parents. They must learn not only to adapt to the baby but also to share one another in a way they probably have not had to before. And though the sharing involves mutual pleasure in getting to know the child, it also involves holding back in one's demands on the other, and seeing someone else become highly important to the other.

Initially the mother experiences what the psychoanalyst D. W. Winnicott calls 'primary maternal preoccupation', a kind of normal illness during which the mother has an enormously heightened sensitivity to the infant's feelings, allowing her to respond quickly and indeed anticipate many of the baby's needs. The child apparently needs this early devotion, which provides him/her with a basis on which to build an enduring self-identity, and an image of a world in which attachment and continuity are possible. Yet during the initial months in which the mother is becoming profoundly attached to the infant, and the infant is absorbing her love and care for future growth, she has little energy available for other interests, and many other demands simply cannot be met. So she is dependent upon others – usually, and ideally, her husband – to protect and support her. This involves offering sympathy with her attachment to the child, and preventing other things from intruding upon her and demanding attention she cannot give. The husband's task is difficult – he has to share her concern

142

with the new child, and help her devote herself to the child, but he himself has little support. He is probably getting less sympathy than usual from his wife, so he may feel excluded from his usual source of emotional energy, and also he may feel excluded from a close relationship with the child, whom he probably loves immensely, but with whom he cannot be as involved as, for example, a nursing mother.

Many things can go wrong in this new triangle. The mother does not magically and inevitably understand her baby's needs. She must learn from her baby, but some parent/infant pairs are better than others at cueing one another. Every parent knows how frustrating it is to have a baby crying inconsolably and not know what is wrong or how to soothe the child. Such crying, if continuous, can raise all sorts of doubts as to one's capacity to parent, or even one's ability to love and to arouse love in the child. Or, if the mother is depressed – and this is not uncommon after the birth of a child – then her own responsiveness and her ability to empathise with others will be suppressed. She will miss her baby's cues, and fail to get to know him/her, and therefore be further isolated and despondent. An anxious parent may overstimulate her child, who may either become frustrated and fussy or, as a defence against the excessive stimulation, lethargic. Just to make all these potential problems worse, the parents are probably physically exhausted. If the mother carries the burden of interrupted nights alone, then the father may not appreciate what a strain it is – yet if he shares the wakeful nights, he may be under the stress of fatigue himself, and therefore be unable to give her emotional support.

The marital friction which can occur at this stage frequently focuses on parents-in-law. Susan wanted to be protected from interference. She was full of doubts as to her ability to mother (having had a poor relationship with her own mother), and the type of 'help' her mother-in-law offered increased those doubts. 'Don't you think he's cold?', she would say, or 'Poor baby, he has a gas bubble. Do you think you drank too much cranberry juice? It can make your milk sour.' The mother-in-law's suggestions and comments and guesses made it difficult for Susan to attend to her infant in her own way. Automatically a mother tries this and that to soothe her child, jiggling it, changing its position, talking to it, distracting it, offering it food or a toy. Unless she feels confident of gauging the success or failure of these attempts (and she has to listen and attend – is he crying louder now? are his muscles more relaxed, even though he is still crying? is the toy catching his interest, or does distraction distress him more?), then background suggestions can be infuriating. Her husband was to some degree sympathetic. He saw there was a cost to his mother's visit. Yet he was proud of his new son, and protective of his mother, who was delighted with her first grandchild and wanted to participate in the initial excitement, and who in fact did help with the housework and would take over for an hour during the day so that Susan could have a rest. Was it too much to ask? He could not understand why it seemed too much for Susan. He felt she was being selfish with the baby. He also felt caught in the tension between his mother and his wife. He could take neither side without offending someone he loved, and no one would take his side.

When Bethan's mother came to stay with her during her convalescence from a Caesarian birth, she was delighted to have someone take over all domestic jobs while she had the luxury of spending all her time with her baby daughter. Bethan's husband, Sam, on the other hand, was immensely irritated as his entire house seemed to be taken over by his mother-in-law. She would answer the door and invite people in. She would invite her own friends and relatives round to tea. His father-in-law would discuss household jobs with the workmen, and suggest this and that to them – not exactly behind his son-in-law's back – it was clearly not intentional, but it was as though Sam no longer had authority in his own home. Between the care provided by his mother-in-law and the time spent by his wife with the child, he was left out of account, too, with the baby, and he was enraged that these first days at home were being taken away from him. Every time he sat down to read a newspaper, his father-in-law would join him, trying to make conversation because the assumption in his wife's family was that people did not want to be left alone – but if Sam could not have time alone with his child, then he wanted to be alone, just to have some reprieve from the frustration of the parents-in-law's presence.

When the first child is born the parent couple, who are learning to cope with sharing one another in a new way, also have to learn to negotiate a new sharing relationship with their parents. It is easier for the new parents to do this than for the new grandparents to relinquish the control they had as parents – both over their children and over their grandchildren – and accept the more familiar, less disciplinary role proper to that of grandparent. Few parents and grandparents relinquish the control or the belief that they should control the young generations. After all, they are used to expressing their love in this way. What was once duty has become a bad habit. Sometimes it irritates their own child more than a son- or daughter-in-law, because the son- or daughter-in-law is more resistant to their methods of control, which are often highly subtle and therefore all the more irritating. Sometimes the son- or daughter-in-law will be quicker to take offence because the parent-in-law's techniques are more obvious, since they are different from those practised in his/her own family; because they are not his/her parents, the child-in-law is more resentful of their claim to authority.

But most grandparents do try to adapt to the new family, if only out of self-protection. The love they have for their grandchildren makes them vulnerable, and a son- or daughter-in-law who wants to hurt a parent-in-law can certainly use this attachment as a weapon. No matter how powerful and well respected a person may be in public life, the power of a parent over a child is paramount, and therefore this power may be used against the grandparent. It has been said that Sanjay Ghandi's widow, Maneka, played a cat-and-mouse game with her mother-in-law, Indira Ghandi. When Sanjay – Indira's favourite son, the son picked out to inherit her position – died, her greatest comfort was in Sanjay's son. Maneka would consent to a meeting, and then cancel it at the last minute. The grandmother, who held so much public power, was powerless in face of the woman who controlled her grandson's life.

Many grandparents are aware of their child-in-law's power. Even if that power does not work against them, they are aware of it, and try to placate the child-in-law because of it. They are like obedient children in face of the child-in-law's instructions over the handling of the grandchild. Yet caution is difficult to sustain, because they feel they have a right to be treated as competent caretakers – have they not raised their own children? So there may well be humiliation in the care they take, and resentment, which of course will be picked up by their child-in-law's critical eye.

Old Wounds and New Battles

If parents have strong negative feelings towards the grandparents, then seeing themselves as parents – which will involve identifying themselves with their parents – may be very difficult. All fears of this kind are aggravated during primary maternal preoccupation because the ego boundaries are blurred. In her devotion and involvement the mother not only is unable to see where she ends and the baby begins, but also has greater difficulty in distinguishing where she ends and her mother begins – or indeed, where she ends and any representative of motherhood, who has influence over her, begins. Because she knows herself to be fragile, the new mother finds intrusion more threatening. Her parents-in-law's offer of 'help' may be more threatening than that of her own parents, because even although her own parents may have more power of intrusion (since she is less fully separate from them anyway), they bring with them a basic acceptance and love and support which she may not find – or believe she has found – in her parents-in-law. In many families one parent/parent-in-law has a tremendous power in implicitly demanding that other members think and feel and act according to a projected image. The birth of a grandchild may stimulate that parent/parent-in-law to assert this with full force, telling the

146

new parents how they will feel, what the child will do or make them do, and what they will do. 'Harry will work harder now, you'll see', Beth told her daughter-in-law. 'His father got down to things after he was born. That little thing will be able to wrap him around her little finger. You won't have to get at him anymore.'

Beth was trying to reassure her daughter-in-law, but if we look at what she was really doing, we see a very different story. First, she was interfering with a very difficult decision the new mother was trying to make – at a time when it would be difficult to make any decision. She was sweeping away the daughter-in-law's deep-seated dissatisfaction with her husband – that he did not take responsibilities seriously, that he made no commitment to his family, that even when his daughter was born he was more concerned with the football match on television than with his wife. She was denying the validity of her daughter-in-law's complaints by saying they would simply disappear. Secondly, she indicated that the baby daughter would succeed where the wife had failed. The 'little thing would be able to wrap him round her little finger', but, admittedly, the wife had had no influence even though – the assumption was – she had been 'getting at him'.

In a host of far more minor ways a parent or parent-in-law accustomed to dictating roles and images will take on a new destructive dimension. In generally controlled families, quarrels emerge because the new mother must fight her mother-in-law in order to assert control over herself. She will not be strong enough to dismiss the mother-in-law's projections. She will have to give her complaints a hearing. Perhaps she believes in the mother-in-law's power, and so seeks to change herself by changing the mother-in-law's image of her.

The family is a system. The fragile autonomy of one member may be reinforced at the expense of another. The mother-in-law who is all charged up to be an excellent grandmother may undermine the performance of the mother. Few visits from grandparents are without some elements of competition for being 'best with the children'. 'I'll get her to eat', my mother-in-law tells me when the children sit down at a meal which my older daughter professes not to like. And she is usually successful. 'I'll get him to wear it', she tells my sister-in-law when her son has been given 'the wrong kind' of bluejeans. Indeed, she is successful where the mothers have failed. Children are more willing to give in to their grand-parents. There is less pride at stake, less benefit to be gained from driving the adult crazy through resistance. The fact that it is not generally the grandparent's job to discipline the child makes the child more amenable to suggestion, as he would be with a playmate. The grandmother who succeeds where the mother fails, however, is likely to make the most of this, taking pride in her handling of the child – when in fact it simply cannot be compared to a parent's handling.

Grandparents' tactics vary, and some point out how well they are doing and how much they are doing by claiming that the child is very difficult. This of course casts criticism on the parents. The child is difficult because the parents do not raise him properly, and the grandparent has taken over a difficult job and worked hard at it and made the most of it. Judy's mother-in-law raises her eyebrows every time Judy's four-year-old son throws a tantrum, and sneaks a conspiratorial glance at her son. Judy is sure she is criticising her for allowing such behaviour, and her mother-in-law's implicit criticism is hardly alleviated by the fact that her husband believes that his mother is 'perfect'. Perfect mothers make devastating mothers-in-law, not only because the wife pales in contrast, but also because she has no support from her hus-band in any battles with the mother-in-law.

To assert her importance, a grandmother may continually remind the family how much she is doing for them – and this may appear not only as long speeches about duty and grati-tude, but in a wealth of tiny detail: 'I'll clear the table for you now' and 'I've just taken out the rubbish', or 'I'll get the tea ready' and 'Have I finally finished putting everything away now? There's so much clutter with young children.' It can go on and on, until the obsessional helpfulness appears aggres-sive, as though the mother-in-law is saying, 'See how much I'm doing for you.' The grandparents, who are so reluctant to relinquish their importance and usefulness in the family, may work hard at poisoning the help they genuinely give.

It is not only the mother and grandparents who change when a new child is brought into the delicate family balance. If the father changes, and old conflicts with his parents are aroused, or if he relives former patterns which for better or worse were practised in his childhood home, then the relationship with his wife, and her relationship with her parents-in-law, will be changed.

There is a tendency for parents to identify with the child of the same sex: the father sees himself in the son, the mother sees herself and judges her life by that of her daughter. Often it is the first child who bears the brunt of the parents' projections, but a child who has the same place in the sibship as the parent (both father and son were the second son, or both mother and daughter have one older brother, for example) may also be the target of parental projection. This is not always negative. Projection involves foresight and sympathy, not only fantasy. The third son in a very large family was given special consideration by his father who himself had been the third son – and in some respects the forgotten or undervalued son, since his older brothers had been particularly bright and apt to realise their father's ambitions. The father saw his older two sons as bright and aggressive – like his older brothers – but because he had felt so left out of his father's affections, he himself found it difficult to be close to the older boys, as though he was still in competition with them. His own father enforced this problem by responding very positively to his older grandsons just as he had to his own older sons (who had been killed in the war). The mother was at a loss to improve the father's relations with their older children, and became despondent as she saw the children becoming arrogant and unruly under the grandfather's protection – for the grandfather was a typical indulgent grandparent; but in default of their real father they had no paternal discipline, and so took advantage of the grandfather. With the instinct at fault-finding that is often quicker than rational justification, the mother turned against her father-in-law and, much to the amazement of her husband (she had been his father's 'favourite daughter-in-law'), forbade the children to have anything more to do with him. The family balance improved, and the restrictions upon the father-in-law in the household were somewhat lifted, but he never forgave his daughter-in-law for seeing him as a harmful influence. His son was able to accept this breach, and to support his wife, because he had himself never had the opportunity to depend upon his father, who had been so attached to the older brothers.

People can try to avoid old family patterns, too, but sometimes this counter-history is as bizarre as a repetition of a previous pattern. When a person has experienced one of those strange coalitions in his or her family of birth, where, for example, one child will join with a parent against the other parent, or against a sibling, he or she will have a good idea of the harm such a 'conspiracy' can do to people on the inside. Favoured children are often self-defeating because they feel guilty about their parents' preference or about their privileges. They may in their adult family be fastidiously even-handed in a way that prevents spontaneity, or they may be recalcitrantly interfering with any one-to-one relationship within the family, because they are excessively suspicious of alliances. The birth of a child may stimulate these fears, and the natural closeness between a parent and his/her child, which is often increased when the child becomes a parent and the parent becomes a grandparent, will be objected to, and may be all the more difficult to tolerate at a time when the new parent must worry about the balance tipped by the new arrival. Or a person who witnessed such a coalition between, say, his brother and mother, may believe that such alliances are inevitable, and he may be quick to form one himself, so as to avoid being on the outside for a second time.

If one partner comes from such a family, then at least one set of parents-in-law/grandparents will be accustomed to this type of family alliance, and the grandchildren will provide new players in their game. The son- or daughter-in-law is more likely to be angered by such manipulations, because he or she is more likely, as an outsider, to notice such things. The parents-in-law may try to minimise the son- or daughter-in-law's influence, often through a type of criticism that is well known to people with in-law problems. Sometimes they will issue a moderate complaint such as 'Your Dad's a funny man. We don't really understand one another', but the criticism may be far more pointed, such as 'Don't do that, or you'll grow up like your father.'

In the post-war study of families in East London, it was found that in-law tension, or rivalry between pairs of grandparents (which would be filtered through the marriage partners) was minimised if priority was given to the wife's parents, especially on important holidays.[2] If it was understood that the wife's parents had the first claim on their daughter and her children at Christmas, a good deal of marital squabbling and trade-offs was avoided. But the only instances in which I found this pattern to hold was in the help a grandparent might offer a parent after the birth of a child. Usually the wife's mother-in-law will step aside for the wife's mother, though the mother-in-law may help from a distance by looking after the older children until the mother and baby are stronger. Only if the wife has quarrelled with her own mother, or if her mother is dead, will the mother-in-law come to help her daughter-in-law with a new baby.

In other circumstances, however, the grandparents' priority was pretty well controlled by the grandparents themselves. The set of parents-in-law most likely to remind a child about remembering a relative's birthday, the set of grandparents most meticulous about sending presents on birthdays, were the parents-in-law most likely to receive them too, and to be visited or invited on family holidays. The reminders about duties owed to other family members, and the careful attention they gave to the married couple and grandchildren on birthdays, tended to act as a highly effective control. The rudeness about gifts received from a parent-in-law ('This tie is so hideous it must be from your mother-in-law'), therefore, not only slights the parent-in-law's choice of gift, but the fact of gift-giving, which may well be seen as a form of blackmail, or a means of manipulation.

Family Myths

A myth can describe a story which may be fictional, but which reveals rather than hides essential truths – or it can describe the falsification of a situation. Family mythology consists of stories told and retold, which influence the family's self-perceptions – or which express and project the identity of a member of the family. Grandparents frequently make contact with their grandchildren through such tales, which usually involve some family history, but which have the effect of perpetuating certain roles or assumptions or outlooks.

'If you eat up all your dinner, then I will tell you a story about your father when he was a little boy', my mother-in-law cajoles her granddaughter.

> Once when your father was a very little boy, and your grandfather was in the navy, I had to prepare a house for some other naval people who were coming to stay there. Your father was so good, that I could let him play outside by himself, even though he was very small. He wanted to pick daisies on the grass outside. I watched him for a minute, and then went back inside, because I had to get on with things. When I next went outside he was nowhere in sight. But I had to stay and wait for the people to arrive. When they came, I said, 'Everything's all ready for you. But I mustn't stop. I must go to the police station and find my little boy'. When I go to the police station there he was, and the policemen said he had been very good.

My husband completes the story. He had followed the grass around the corner, until the house his mother was tidying was out of view. A woman had found him and asked if he knew where he was, and he said 'no', so she offered to take him home. He knew his address, and he gave it to her, and she took him to his house by bus, but no one was in, so she took him to the police station, where his mother found him.

My sister-in-law and I have been fascinated by this story. We reckon that my husband must have been less than three at the time, because she was not yet born – yet he was allowed to play alone outside. Also, we try to calculate the time he was unattended. He had had time to get lost, to be found by a woman, who took him home on a bus, and who then took him to a police station. We are also amazed by the fact that she stayed at the house, waiting for the people to arrive, even after she knew her son was missing. So what this often repeated story suggests is that they are a very lucky family, that their world is controlled, that people will befriend them. It also suggests that the children are very 'good' even when they are getting into mischief. It is a re-telling of what must have been a gruelling experience, but it denies any anxiety or any guilt, for the point of it is that the family will be fine, that it lives in a very nice world.

Many family myths are far more intriguing than this one. Sometimes they create dashing grandfathers, who were admirals or pioneers or explorers. Lynn, as a child, heard stories from her grandfather about his life on the Canadian frontier, and she is convinced that these stories prevented her from seeing her life as bound by the provincial and domestic outlook of her mother. But these tales can stunt, too. Pamela was outraged to hear her mother-in-law tell stories to her child about relatives with 'bad blood', and in particular, about an uncle who had cast aside his mother and become dissolute and criminal as, too early, he sought his independence. It seemed to her the type of story that would make her children afraid when they began to strive for independence. The son or daughter will have heard the stories so many times that they seem harmless. The son- or daughter-in-law will usually be quicker at spotting the secret or unconscious beliefs and attitudes which the stories perpetuate. Their irritation may be expressed as simple bordeom ('Oh, there he goes again with that old story'), but the real objection will be to the attempted manipulation of the family identity.

Trusting Care

An elderly grandfather, who had adored animals in his youth,
insisted that he take his four-year-old grandson to Lincoln
Zoo. 'I've always looked forward to this', he said. When his
daughter-in-law expressed concern at how taxing such an
outing would be for a man who had recently been ill, her
mother-in-law countered, 'He looked after your husband when
he was small. You think we know nothing about children?'
The mother relented. The active child scrambled over the
barrier between the public walkway and the rocks of the lions'
enclosure, fell and was killed.

Grandparents are not parents. They have not been trained
by daily contact with the toddler to anticipate his or her
antics, and they might not be quick enough to deal with them.
Some grandparents know this, and are very good at gauging
their limits. Judy's parents-in-law looked after her young son
when she and her husband went on holiday. She requested
various parents of her son's friends to contact her parents-in-
law while she was away, and to make arrangements for her
son to play with their children, because she feared that he
would otherwise be too isolated. These parents obliged her,
and tried to arrange for her son to play with their children, but
the grandmother persistently rebuffed them. 'I don't know
you', she would declare. 'I'm not the mother. I can't decide to
trust someone else's child with you.'

At face value her behaviour is highly insulting not merely to
the other parents, but also to Judy, who had requested that
her son be allowed to play with their children, and told her
mother-in-law that she had made these requests. Was not her
mother-in-law simply ignoring her assessment of these parents?
And was she not gratuitously alienating her daughter-in-law's
friends? But the justification for this rudeness lay in the grandmother's knowledge of her own limits. If she was to look after
her young grandson then she had to be in control. The
company of a friend would stimulate him to a point she might
not be able to handle. 'I am not the mother' sounded like a
strange argument to the parents who wanted the son to play

154

with their children, but it was a just statement about her position as caretaker. She had to be more careful with another person's child, but she also had to be particularly careful with herself. She must not stretch her capacities, which were not as flexible and as sturdy as those of a mother.

Grandparents, if able, have a right to help. It is a way of participating in the lives of their children and grandchildren, and a way of continuing to make themselves useful at a time when they may well feel on the periphery. A grandmother whose neighbours had been complaining to the social services because she kept asking them to shop for her, to change a light bulb, to make a doctor's appointment for her, and then to take her to the doctor's surgery, was judged unable to live alone, and the only family member with enough room to take her in was her son. As soon as she moved in to her son and daughter-in-law's home, her helplessness increased. She became obviously resentful towards her daughter-in-law, who did her best to cater to every whim, and she became depressed. Eventually, with the help of a therapist, she expressed her desire to help out in the home – to cook a meal when her daughter-in-law had to be out late or was tired. She had felt her presence was tedious to her grandchildren, who were young adolescents, and she tried to find ways to help out – perhaps by doing their domestic jobs for them when they wanted to go out. Once her daughter-in-law ceased to look after her like an invalid, she felt she was a bona fide member of the household, and no longer under her daughter-in-law's control.

Happy Endings

Parents-in-law generally do become grandparents, and this provides a central common interest. Usually the love for the grandchild that the grandparents share with the son- or daughter-in-law is more important than the minor and multitudinous moves in family politics. Most people eventually come to terms with their in-laws by 'accepting them for what they are', which, I suppose, means not so much not trying to change them as not resenting them – or perhaps being able to ignore certain aspects of them. Eventually, too, in-laws tend to reach an equilibrium in their expectations of one another. At the outset, in-laws can differ widely as to how they approach one another. One person may believe that an in-law is a family member, and should be loved and honoured accordingly. Someone else may see an in-law not as a family member, but as a relative of his or her spouse, and therefore not as someone to whom love is automatically owed, but rather as someone who deserves an extra special chance at friendship and appreciation. After a time these differences, which may well be jarring, settle down, and each gets used to the other's assumptions.

The benefits of making concessions and getting on are, most people find, enormous. The parents-in-law benefit because the grandchildren can respond to them without prejudice, or without guilt at possible disloyalty to one of their parents. The couple themselves benefit because resentment towards in-laws inevitably spills into the marriage, and it does the marriage good to overcome it, or at least to contain it. The antagonistic parties themselves benefit because bad feelings harboured towards in-laws are unpleasant to have. But have them we do, and now we may begin to understand them.

Notes and References

Chapter 2

1. J. Goody, *The Development of the Family and Marriage in Europe* (Cambridge University Press, 1983) p. 270.
2. H. Hallam, *View of the State of Europe during the Middle Ages* (London: Alex Murray and Son, 1868) p. 456.
3. J. Goody, *The Development of the Family, passim.*
4. Bruno Bettelheim, *The Uses of Enchantment* (New York: A. Knopf, 1976).
5. *Express News Service*, Dehli, 5 July 1983.
6. M. Fortes, 'Kinship and Marriage among the Ashanti', in A.R. Radcliffe-Brown and D. Forde (eds), *African Systems of Kinship and Marriage* (London: Oxford University Press, 1950).
7. Judson T. Landis and Mary G. Landis, *Building a Successful Marriage* (New York: Prentice Hall, 1948).
8. P. Willmott and M. Young, *Family and Kinship in East London* (London: Routledge & Kegan Paul, 1957).

Chapter 3

1. Henry Dicks, *Marital Tensions* (London: Routledge & Kegan Paul, 1967) p. 66; see also Jay Haley, 'Marriage Therapy', *Archives of General Psychiatry*, 8 (March 1963) 213–34.

2. Robert Skynner and John Cleese, *Families, and How to Survive Them* (London: Methuen, 1983).

3. Patrick Wright, *A Tale of Two Mothers-in-Law* (London: Heinemann, 1983).

Chapter 4

1. Henry Dicks, *Marital Tensions*.

2. Jay Haley, 'Marriage Therapy', p. 224.

3. Ibid.

4. Lily Pincus and Christopher Dare, *Secrets in the Family* (London: Faber, 1978).

5. J. Byng-Hall, 'Symptom Bearer as Marital Distance Regulator', *Family Process*, 19 (1980) 355–65.

6. Lily Pincus and Christopher Dare, *Secrets in the Family*, discuss a similar case, p. 42.

Chapter 5

1. Peter Blos, *On Adolescence* (New York: The Free Press of Glencoe, 1962) p. 178.

2. Patrick Wright, *Two Mothers-in-Law*.

3. *The Times*, 6 April 1984.

4. Cf. David Halberstam, *The Powers that Be* (London: Chatto & Windus, 1979) pp. 283 ff.

Chapter 6

1. J. Lewis *et al.*, *No Single Thread: Psychological Health in Family Systems* (New York: Brunner/Mazel, 1976).

Chapter 8

1. Willmott and Young, *Family and Kinship in East London*.

2. Ibid., p. 17.

3. Ibid., p. 46.

4. Ibid., p. 158.

5. Peter Townsend, *Family Life of Old People* (London: Routledge & Kegan Paul, 1957) p. 25.

6. Ibid., p. 85.

7. Ibid.

8. Peter Marris, *Widows and Their Families* (London: Routledge & Kegan Paul, 1958) p. 79.

9. Ibid., p. 80.

10. Andrew Cherlin, *Marriage, Divorce, Remarriage* (Cambridge, Mass.: Harvard University Press, 1981) p. 108.

11. Reported to me by therapist Philippa Comber of Churchill College, Cambridge.

Chapter 9

1. A. R. Radcliffe-Brown and D. Forde (eds), *African Systems of Kinship*, p. 30.
2. P. Willmott and M. Young, *Family and Kinship in East London*, p. 42.

Selected Bibliography

Abdullah, T. A. and S. Zeidenstein, S., *Village Women of Bangladesh: Prospects for Change* (Oxford: Pergamon Press, 1981).

Bentovim, A., Gorell Barnes, G., Cooklin, A. (eds), *Family Therapy* (London: The Institute of Family Therapy, 1982).

Blos, Peter, *On Adolescence* (New York: The Free Press of Glencoe, 1962).

Boszormenyi-Nagy, I. and Spark, G. M., *Invisible Loyalties* (Hagerstown: Harper & Row, 1973).

Bowen, M., 'Family Therapy after Twenty Years', *American Handbook of Psychiatry*, 5, Arieti, S. (ed.), (New York: Basic Books, 1975).

Bowen, M., 'The Use of Family Therapy in Clinical Practice', *Comprehensive Psychiatry*, 7: 345 (1966).

Bowen, M., 'Towards the Differentiation of a Self in One's Own Family', *Family Interaction*, Framo, L. J. (ed.), (New York: Springer, 1972).

Byng-Hall, J., 'Symptom Bearer as Marital Distance Regulator', *Family Process*, 19 (1980) 355–65.

Cherlin, Andrew, *Marriage, Divorce, Remarriage* (Cambridge, Mass.: Harvard University Press, 1981).

Dicks, Henry, *Marital Tensions* (London: Routledge & Kegan Paul, 1967).

Elikin, A. P., *The Australian Aborigines* (Sydney: Angus and Robertson, 1964).

Epstein, Scarlett T. and Watts, Rosemary A. (eds), *The Endless Day* (Oxford: Pergamon Press, 1981).

Firth, Raymond, Hubert, Jane, Forge, Anthony, *Families and Their Relatives* (London: Routledge & Kegan Paul, 1970).

Fortes, M., *The Web of Kinship among the Tallensi* (London: Oxford University Press, 1949).

Freud, Sigmund, *Totem and Taboo* (New York: Random House, 1918).

Goody, J., *The Development of the Family and Marriage in Europe* (Cambridge University Press, 1983).

Bibliography

Grinker, Roy, 'On Identification', *The International Journal of Psychoanalysis*, 38, 6 (1957) 1–12.

Haley, J., 'Marriage Therapy', *Archives of General Psychiatry*, 8 (March 1963) 213–34.

Hiatt, L. R., 'Your Mother-in-law is Poison', *Man*, (N. S.) 19 (1984) 183–98.

Jones, E., 'The Phantasy of the Reversal of Generations', *Papers on Psychoanalysis*, ch. XXIII, 5th edn (London: Bailliére, Tindall and Cox, 1950).

Kirkpatrick, Clifford, *The Family as Process and Institution*, 2nd edn (New York: Roland Press, 1963).

Kuper, A., *Anthropologists and Anthropology* (Harmondsworth: Allen Lane, 1973).

Lewis, J. et al., *No Single Thread: Psychological Health in Family Systems* (New York: Brunner/Mazel, 1976).

Marris, Peter, *Widows and their Families* (London: Routledge & Kegan Paul, 1958).

Mead, Margaret, *Sex and Temperament* (London: Routledge & Kegan Paul, 1935).

Minuchin, Salvador, *Families and Family Therapy* (Cambridge, Mass.: Harvard University Press, 1974).

Mukhopadhyay, Maitrayee, *Silver Shackles* (Oxford: Oxfam, 1984).

Paolino, Thomas and McCrady, Barbara S., *Marriage and Marital Therapy* (New York: Brunner/Mazel, 1978).

Pincus, L. (ed), *Marriage: Studies in Emotional Conflict and Growth* (London: Methuen, 1966).

Pincus, Lily and Dare, Christopher, *Secrets in the Family* (London: Faber, 1978).

Radcliffe-Brown, A. R., and Forde, D. (eds), *African Systems of Kinship and Marriage* (London: Oxford University Press, 1950).

Rey, Manisha, *Bengali Women* (Chicago University Press, 1972).

Schneider, David, *American Kinship: A Cultural Account* (Englewood Cliffs, N. J.: Prentice-Hall, 1968).

Skynner, Robin, *One Flesh: Separate Persons* (London: Constable, 1976).

Skynner, Robin and Cleese, John, *Families, and How to Survive Them* (London: Methuen, 1983).

Stack, Carol B., *All Our Kin* (New York: Harper & Row, 1974).

Townsend, Peter, *Family Life of Old People* (London: Routledge & Kegan Paul, 1957).

Willmott, P. and Young, M., *Family and Kinship in East London* (London: Routledge & Kegan Paul, 1957).

Winnicott, D. W., *The Family and Individual Development* (London: Tavistock Publications, 1961).

Winnicott, D. W., 'Primary Maternal Preoccupation', *Collected Papers: Through Pediatrics to Psychoanalysis* (New York: Basic Books, 1975).

Wright, Patrick, *A Tale of Two Mothers-in-Law* (London: Heinemann, 1983).